Teaching Higher Education to Lead

Teaching Higher Education to Lead

Strategies for the Digital Age

Sam Choon-Yin

Teaching Higher Education to Lead: Strategies for the Digital Age

Copyright © Business Expert Press, LLC, 2022.

Cover design by Charlene Kronstedt

Interior design by Exeter Premedia Services Private Ltd., Chennai, India

All rights reserved. No part of this publication may be reproduced, stored in a retrieval system, or transmitted in any form or by any means—electronic, mechanical, photocopy, recording, or any other except for brief quotations, not to exceed 400 words, without the prior permission of the publisher.

First published in 2021 by
Business Expert Press, LLC
222 East 46th Street, New York, NY 10017
www.businessexpertpress.com

ISBN-13: 978-1-63742-163-5 (paperback)
ISBN-13: 978-1-63742-164-2 (e-book)

Business Expert Press Collaborative Intelligence Collection

Collection ISSN: 2691-1779 (print)
Collection ISSN: 2691-1795 (electronic)

First edition: 2021

10 9 8 7 6 5 4 3 2 1

Description

Competition to provide education is tense, attributed to the ease to access and process information. Technological development has also landed a terrible blow to the employment situation, which forces the higher education institutions to review what and how their students learn. Yet, the desire to retain and grow the number of students and gain commercially can sometimes cloud judgment of educational leaders. They need to know that poorly made decisions hurt the businesses and students.

In this book, Sam Choon-Yin links technological development to demand for education, credentials of university education, jobs, teaching, and learning; and touches on issues of strategies and higher education policies for the digital age. The author provides a critical outlook on the prevailing practices of the higher education institutions. By drawing our attention to the various challenges, the author shows how teaching and learning can be effectively carried out in the digital age to serve the needs of students and hiring companies and ultimately the institutions of higher learning. Understanding the issues and challenges means better design of the curriculum and methods of delivery of the curriculum. At a deeper level, the book raises a complex question of "what makes an education institution different" as they aim to define themselves by fulfilling students' desire. Understanding these issues forms the basis of power for higher education institutions to remain competitive and relevant in the age of digitization.

Keywords

higher education; leadership; digitalization

Contents

Testimonials ix
Preface xi

Chapter 1   University Education—Then, Now, and the Future 1
Chapter 2   Credentials of Higher Education Qualifications 19
Chapter 3   Jobs and Technology 35
Chapter 4   Staying Relevant in the Digital Age 51
Chapter 5   Passion for Learning 69
Chapter 6   Learning in the Digital Age 87
Chapter 7   Good to Great Teachers 107
Chapter 8   Leadership in Higher Education 125

Epilogue 145
References 155
About the Author 169
Index 171

Testimonials

"Dr. Sam Choon-Yin has produced a well-researched, insightful and comprehensive book, which is essential reading for anyone with a serious interest in higher education."—**Sajid Anwar, Professor of Finance, School of Business and Creative Industries, University of the Sunshine Coast**

"There are many stakeholders in higher education, including students, teachers, education institutions, parents, employers, regulators—and they all have a role to play in shaping developments in the education sector. While highly competitive, the education sector is also changing rapidly, particularly in the digital age and during the COVID-19 pandemic. In this book, which I strongly recommend to readers, Sam Choon-Yin takes a strategic perspective in sharing his views and proposes strategies for higher education institutions to lead this development from good to great."—**Lau Chee Kwong, Dean, Associate Professor of Accounting, Nottingham University Business School, University of Nottingham Malaysia**

"In writing this fascinating book, Choon-Yin was clearly inspired to share his experience and insights about the unfolding challenges and issues of education, particularly the unprecedented universal impact that the COVID-19 pandemic had on the pursuit and delivery of higher education. In the unfolding digital world, and the frenetic pace of digitalisation of teaching and learning, administrators, educators, teachers and students have all had to adapt with the explosion of knowledge and the ensuing ways of delivering innovative learning. Choon-Yin wisely forewarns that, notwithstanding the ethical and commercial imperatives of managing financially viable tertiary Institutions, the fundamentals of reading, learning, teaching excellence, passion for lifelong learning must not be lost sight of in the digital age."—**Karmjit Singh, Chairman, Chartered Institute of Logistics and Transport (Singapore)**

Preface

For more than two decades, I have gained experience in the higher education sector as an educator and an administrator. I have also thought about strategy; carried out research in higher education; and been interacting with parents, educators, government officials, auditors, and researchers. I have benefited immensely from these involvements. Out of the experience as an educator and administrator that I have gathered over the years, I have written books and articles.

To me, writing is always a more challenging task as compared to reading. With an idea and a body of information, I spend a lot of time deciding how to put the materials together to develop meaningful parts to suit the kind of audience I have in mind. For readers who are directly involved in the higher education sector, I hope that you will find the book useful. I also have in mind readers who are nonspecialists thereby the use of technical language has been avoided as much as possible.

Education is a multifaceted phenomenon, and it cannot be covered comprehensively in a single volume. I have a modest aim when I set myself the task in writing this book. I want to highlight the key issues in the higher education sector and offer some suggestions as to how educators and administrators can overcome the challenges for the post-pandemic world. These are big issues. I hope I have not simplified too much. The points raised in this book are meant to illustrate my points, not to substitute other records, which I try to give readers access to fuller accounts in the footnotes.

The issues raised in this book are certainly not the only ones that matter. George Orwell has said that the subject matter chosen by the author is often determined by the age and events taking place in the lives of the author. I have selected issues that are of particular interest to me. There is an issue related to the demand side of education system. Many still see education as a passport to good life and good job. While working the way up may sound fascinating and attractive, it seems that many of those who start at the bottom of the ladder never manage to climb high enough and therefore remain at the bottom. That is why it pays to acquire higher educational qualification to enable individuals to climb up the corporate ladder step by step, avoid falling off the ladder and if they are laid off, to bounce back by securing a new job.

Our brain is particularly sensitive to relative differences and changes. As more and more pursue higher education in order to get ahead, others with fewer skills and less qualification are worse off and decide to get on the bandwagon themselves. Seeing what higher education can do for others strike the mind of those without the qualification to do something about it. They know what they are missing. The world has been marked with growing number of graduates bringing the concern of overeducation into the agenda of many governments.

The question on the purpose of education has been raised countless times (see the chapter on "University Education—Then, Now, and the Future"). One way of answering this question is to consider what students demand of education and want to achieve with it. Ultimately, students strive for happiness. Achieving this comes in two forms: a positive and a negative endeavor. On the one hand, students aim to reap strong pleasure and experience, and on the other hand, students aim for the absence of displeasure and disappointment.

Getting a degree is not a bad option. Higher education educates students to be lifelong and critical learners, and there are individuals who pursue higher education simply because of their love for learning as I have documented in the chapter on "Passion for Learning."

But when university programs are seen to train students for their job, issues can arise if the universities neglect or are reluctant to catch up with the industry requirements. I am getting concerned that a degree might not necessarily improve one's readiness for work. Good grades are so easy to come by that they are rendered useless in assessing the suitability of candidates in the hiring process. More companies are relying on noneducational credentials to determine who to hire. I discuss this issue in the chapter on "Credentials of Higher Education Qualifications."

I am fascinated by the way technology has transformed the education sector. Technology has always been in the news, affecting our thinking on nearly every subject. Education, to a very considerable extent, has responded to technological development from the invention of writing and movable printers down to computers and the Internet.

Technological development, coupled with globalization, has landed a terrible blow to the employment situation (see the chapter on "Jobs and Technology"). The manufacturing jobs have seen a steady decline. Robots and machines have replaced routine work, forcing unskilled and semiskilled manual workers into lower paid service sector jobs. What remains in manufacturing is high skilled in advanced technology industries. The climate of economic insecurity and the fear of getting laid off have led many people to question the merits of technology advancement. Although the job losses may be balanced by gains in other industries of the economy workers cannot easily get hired because they lack the necessary skills or cannot relocate, creating financial hardship and loss of self-esteem. However, it is also worth noting that labor saving technologies are not available to every company at the reasonable cost. Small employers are also less flexible to embrace technology.

For education providers who see preparing their students for the job market as their key role, offering courses that are deemed relevant to the employers, and instilling soft skills that employers want are important considerations. Higher education providers need to teach their students how to think, identify issues of a particular situation, and decide the action to take so as to distinguish themselves as truly effective learner. This is often not the case. Higher education providers have been accused of offering courses that are too theoretical, too specialized and lacked relevance to the job market. There are others who have accused higher education institutions of dumbing down the curriculum and inflating students' grades just so that they can attract and retain students. Critics have argued that higher education is overpriced and is wasting the time and energy of teens.

As new businesses and industries emerge in the post-pandemic economy, how should the curriculum be altered to cater to the needs of the society? Should institutions of higher learning transit from a single discipline solution to a multidisciplinary approach? What makes an education institution great is not to predict the actual jobs and technology that will emerge. What education providers ought to do is to develop the capacity to act, understand where technology is likely to have a major impact on students and teachers, and the ability to take advantage of technological change to do things better. I address these questions in the chapter on "Staying Relevant in the Digital Age."

Technological advancements have also impacted student learning. Students today find simulation so readily available in the digital age that they cannot pay attention to a particular activity like reading a book for more than 15 minutes before needing to transition to other activities: watching a video, playing games, and so on. Edward Swing, Douglas Gentile, and their team conducted studies on the effects of video games on school children level of attention and found that those who had more than two hours of screen time per day on television and video games were more likely to develop attention problem.[1] For digital natives, the abundance of information does not feel like an overload. They confront a problem of natural limits of attention and ability to absorb information. Susan Greenfield reported that persons who spend considerable amount of time on their digital devices are more likely to develop autistic-like traits like avoiding eye and human contact with others, especially strangers.[2]

Education providers have to know how to deal with students who are so preoccupied with digital devices. Teachers have to be mindful that students can easily access online databases and reading materials, but they still have to read the documents and ask the right questions. With the Internet, schools have been empowered, benefiting from a wide variety of teachers' resources without investing in their creation. As I argue in the chapters on "Learning in the Digital Age" and "Good to Great Teachers,"

---

[1] Swing, Gentile, Anderson, and Walsh, "Television and Videogame Exposure and the Development of Attention Problem." In a related study, Gentile and Swing found that children who had attentional problem spent more time in playing videogames, suggesting a bidirectional relationship between gaming and attentional problem. See Gentile, Swing, Lim, and Khoo, "Videogames Playing, Attention Problems, and Impulsiveness: Evidence of Bidirectional Causality." There are others who did not find videogames as significant predictor of children's attentional problem (correlation of 0.03) as compared to increased aggression (r = 0.06), reduced prosocial behavior (r = 0.04). See, for example, Ferguson, "The Influence of Television and Video Game Use on Attention and School Problems"; Ferguson, "Do Angry Birds Make for Angry Children?"

[2] Greenfield, "Mind Change," p. 131.

to prepare students for the future of work, teachers must embrace and use the technology. They should see the Internet as a supplementary tool to make teaching more fun and engaging to students. In these two chapters, I suggest ways for teachers to help students succeed in their studies.

As educators, we are affected by the brain power of the people we teach. It is therefore essential that we understand how the human brain works and how learning takes place. We must act to the best of our ability, using our skills and knowledge to guide our students. As elaborated in the chapter on "Learning in the Digital Age," there must be room to recognize our students' differences in aptitude and ability, to rectify their mistakes and produce an effect on their mind, and to alter their behavior for their own benefit. It is a challenge that we must accept. If accepted and the attempt fails, at least we have done our best that any existing human being is capable of approaching it. We can learn from the experience and do even better the next time when we encounter similar situations.

Besides technology, I am intrigued with the expansion of markets in the education sector. Education institutions are being implicated in the shift toward money and markets that are once governed by nonmarket norms. Imagine paying cash to someone to write essays or complete coursework on your behalf, or imagine paying students to improve academic performance or reward teachers with salary bonuses for each student who passes the examinations. Something is lost when education is turned into a market community. Michael Sandel wrote about the consequences in his book *What Money Can't Buy*. One consequence is unfairness. Consider a university that auctions seats to the highest bidders. Because the number of seats is limited, offering seats to the highest bidders reduces the number of seats for others, depriving students with the greatest talent and promise and eroding the integrity of the university and value of its qualifications. The other consequence is corruption. Putting a price on education corrupts the individual. Paying the students to read, wrote Sandel, "might get them to read more, but also teach them to regard reading as a chore rather than a source of intrinsic satisfaction."[3]

The fact is that higher education institutions are confounded with multiple objectives: to be a leader in scientific research, to excel in

---

[3] Sandel, "What Money Can't Buy," p. 9.

teaching, to provide the best learning experience to students, and the mission dictates the allocation of resources and policies administered by the institutions. If the focus is to be the leader in scientific research, universities with heavy research funds and the ability to recruit research-oriented faculty are more likely to win. If the goal is to deliver the best learning experience to students, universities with a heavy focus on teaching excellence is more likely to excel. If the focus is on the size of the intake, then the universities may devise the admission policy to admit students based on portfolios and rely less on academic measures like test scores and position in class. In an era in which universities compete fiercely for students domestically and internationally, will universities have the backbone to be selective in admitting students and turn away potential students? Will the faculty be willing to spend more time on student consultation and teaching to support the cause or voice for their displeasure over "downgrading" of the quality of education?

The introduction of markets changes the characteristics of education. When education is seen as a commodity, education providers run the risk of lowering academic standard and rigor, for example, by dumbing down the curriculum to lower attrition rate and increase student enrolment.

Education providers in this regard need responsible leaders. What do I mean by responsible leadership? On one end, it includes the things that educational leaders should not do. Naturally, this includes illegal actions like bribery, fraud, and failing to comply with rules and regulations. The other end concerns what educational leaders should do, which includes integrity in internal and external communication in dealing with stakeholders, upholding the academic standard and rigor, maintaining safety for students and staff, and managing conflicts between students and the institution. Then, there are the gray areas of student recruitment and sales tactics and disclosure of information to students, parents, and the general public, which can get more complicated as the institution tries to balance multiple objectives. How should the higher education institutions balance the educational and commercial goals to avoid the awkward situation where commercial interest overrides everything else? In the chapter on "Leadership in Higher Education," I argue that ethical decision must be derived from within the organization and championed by the leaders.

Let me conclude this introductory chapter by thanking the persons who have helped me in the pursuit of writing this book. The book owes much to the exchanges I have with my colleagues at PSB Academy. I have benefited immensely from discussions with Viva Sinniah, Derrick Chang, Karuppiah Balamurugan, Rosan Basha, Vincent Chong, Sally Choo, Melissa Liow, Charles Ong, Vijyah Shanmugam, Ramachandran Subramaniyan, Pearly Wong, and Cecilia Yeoh. My sincere appreciation to Boby Sebastian Kappan, Kate Tan, and Seah Seng Wee for reading parts of the book. In writing this book, I have consulted a large number of materials, which have been dutifully checked as far as possible. Should there be evidence of misrepresentation of opinions, facts and others, I would be delighted to make the necessary revisions at the first opportunity. I remain conscious of the fact that there is still much I do not know about education in general and higher education in particular. Unavoidably, my ignorance will show up in pages in this book. Any mistakes of errors are solely mind and should not attributed to my colleagues and institution that I am affiliated with. I also want to express my gratitude to the team at Business Expert Press for their editorial and production work.

Writing this book would not have been possible without the encouragement from my wife, Shiau Hong, and our two children, Mun Wing and Wai Lok. I would like to thank each of them for their love and support. To my mother, Choo Lai Har, thank you for taking care of the family throughout the years. This book is dedicated to her.

CHAPTER 1

University Education—Then, Now, and the Future

Typically, an individual spends more than 10 years in schools before acquiring a higher education qualification. Postsecondary education, as some might call it, includes apprenticeships, vocational education, and pursuit of undergraduate and postgraduate degrees at the institutes of higher learning. Giving the children access to postsecondary education, especially at the university, is part of the parent's dream. Getting a degree is often considered as a passport to a good life. Beyond material gains, university education enables the students to increase their awareness of the nation and culture, and refinement of the self.

This chapter narrates the purposes of education, from the training of clerics to maintain law and order to the training of students to enter the workforce. I argue that general and multidisciplinary education is important to introduce students to a variety of disciplines. Higher education institutions around the world were deeply affected when the coronavirus pandemic hit in the late 2019 and early 2020. I conclude with some thoughts on the role of education in the postpandemic world.

Early Universities

Early schools of higher learning in post-Antiquity Europe existed in Greece and continued into the Roman Empire. In *Scribes and Scholars,* Leighton Reynolds and Nigel Wilson wrote "Schools can be traced at Alexandria, Antioch, Athens, Beirut, Constantinople, and Gaza; they were in effect the universities of the ancient world."[1] At Alexandria, Aristotle was one of the main topics of study. The chief subject at Beirut

---

[1] Reynolds and Wilson, "*Scribes and Scholars,*" p. 45.

was law. The demand for such institutions was attributed to the increase in the Roman civil service in the fourth century.

The oldest existing and continually operating educational institution in the world—the University of Karueein or the University of al-Qarawiyyin—was founded in 859 AD in Fez, Morocco. The university was founded at the beginning of the Islamic Golden Age, which saw the period of cultural, economic, and scientific expansion in the history of Islam, traditionally dated from the 8th to 14th century.[2] The study of classics continued during the glorious years of Islamic civilization that stretched from Spain to China, India, and other parts of Asia.

The Arabs were fascinated by the civilization of the ancient Greeks and translated the Greeks' works. Jack Goody pointed out that the Muslims established madrasas throughout the Muslim world in the 10th and 11th century, and there were significant parallels between the education system in Islam and the Christian West, noting that "the medieval university owed much to the collegiate institution of Arab education."[3] Influences include the Arabic numerals and the study of medicine that the West had fallen behind "due to ban on dissection, on cutting up the human body" and absence of medical texts. These were later brought back to the West by the many translations by the Muslim world.[4]

Education and religion are inseparable in a large measure. For Muslims, the purpose of education is to inculcate Islamic values, determining how one should eat, wash, and live. In most of the Muslim world, education starts with the teaching of the Quran. Religion is so inherent among Muslims that theology and philosophy are indistinguishable. The Jesuits have preached the Gospel and maintained a vast educational network, shaping Catholic church, society, and politics around the world. Humans embrace cultivation guided by faith.

Monasteries in medieval Italy, Ireland, England, and Spain were largely concerned with training ministers, lawyers, and teachers to conduct affairs of the soul and society. The monks were convinced that to be

---

[2] See Rezaeian, "*Muslim World's Universities*"; Guessoum and Osama, "*Revive Universities of the Muslim World.*"
[3] Goody, "*The Thief of History,*" p. 228.
[4] Ibid., p. 296.

good Christians, one must do good, and to do so, the person needed skills and knowledge. They gathered and studied ancient scrolls and manuscripts and imparted the know-how to others. Education was done for the glory of God to prepare the young to embrace intelligently the teachings and directions of the churches. They thought minimal modern language, modern history, or modern literature, but those who were trained frequently advised the Christian Kings to write laws and compose letters to other Kings.

The first university in Europe, the University of Bologna, was established in Italy in around 1088. The university gathered a large number of students and spectators who longed for knowledge. Many camped for days to gain access to lectures and talks conducted by the masters. England forbade students from travelling to other countries, compelling scholars and students to gather at Oxford and culminating in the establishment of the University of Oxford in around 1096 (making it the second oldest university in the world) and Cambridge University in 1209.[5] After the establishment of the University of Oxford and Cambridge University, there was a gap of 600 years before a new university was created in England—the University College London in 1809.[6]

In the case of China, education was in large measure based on the Confucian doctrine, established more than 2,000 years ago. The purpose of education was to prepare candidates for the civil service examinations. The content was therefore purely literary and required mastery of Confucian thought. Candidates would study the classical texts of the tradition and sit for a series of examinations. Only by passing the examinations

---

[5] In 1167, England's Henry II forbade English students to study abroad. Students gathered at Oxford instead. Colleges with dormitories were built after students and local townspeople clashed violently. The colleges were under the supervision of masters. Many of the colleges remain open today. The colleges, wrote Kevin Carey, "were largely autonomous, raised their own money, and were responsible for teaching and student life. The university administered exams and granted degrees." See Carey, "*The End of College*," p. 19.

[6] The long period of the wait was not because of the lack of demand, David Willett explained. It was because of strong barriers to entry. "Oxford and Cambridge had imposed a bar on their graduates' teaching elsewhere in the country to stop the creation of new universities." Willetts, "*A University Education*," p. 17.

they could become administrators, which would typically bring status, titles, positions, and wealth to the candidates.

Education in ancient China did not encourage sufficiently any technical knowledge or skills that would be useful to govern the country. Reformers like Kang Youwei and Liang Qichao viewed the education process as long and time wasting and discouraged the candidates from thinking of original ideas. According to Marianne Bastid, the arrival of western troops in the 19th century prompted China to review its education system. Western power was thought to have been derived from "western knowledge," which consisted of the teaching of science and technological skills. In 1895, China attempted to envisage an education system that would embrace the teaching of science, technological skills, law, and arts. In 1904, the Manchu reform effort included the establishment of a national school system, and in 1905, the abolishment of traditional civil service examinations.[7]

In India, several monasteries like Nalanda were premier tertiary education during the 8th and 12th centuries. Nalanda, a Buddhist center of learning, attracted students from all over Asia, including the great Buddhist monks from Tang China—Xuanzhang and Yijing—to study Buddhism and translate Sanskrit documents into Chinese. With the arrival of the British, things changed. After the Indian uprising in 1857–1858, the British took away the universities' endowments, and three years later "they were all dead."[8] While colleges were set up under British colonial rule (e.g., the Delhi College in 1825), the dropout rate was high. The British left India with a literacy rate of only 16 percent, and a female literacy rate of a mere 8 percent in 1947. Shashi Tharoor argued that those who graduated had a better command of the English language, but they served only their British masters. Therefore, the English language "was not a deliberate gift to India" but "an instrument of colonialism, imparted to Indians only to facilitate the tasks of the English."[9]

---

[7] See Bastid, "*Educational Reform in Early 20th Century China.*"
[8] As mentioned by Frank Griffel, a professor of religious studies from Yale University. Quoted in Baggini, "*How the World Thinks,*" p. 4.
[9] Tharoor, "*Inglorious Empire,*" p. 186.

Early universities in the United States trained clergy and rooted in particular Christian sects, serving mainly wealthy white men. Knowledge production has been a trajectory from the top-down. Early American colleges (such as Harvard—1636, Princeton—1746, Columbia—1754, Brown—1764, and Rutgers—1766) were modeled after the English's college, prescribing medieval courses such as Latin, Greek, Mathematics, Logic, and Moral Philosophy. John Henry Newman who wrote *The Idea of a University* considered knowledge as the key condition of expansion of the mind to allow students to come into contact with modes of thought and various interests and views, which was not possible with a narrow mind and little knowledge.[10] Newman did not regard research as a proper function of a university. The ideal university teaches universal knowledge on a great many subjects, implying that the purpose of education is on the one hand intellectual and on the other hand, to diffuse and extend knowledge. In the course of education, a student acquires measures of quality like honesty, amiability, perseverance, and loyalty by reading classics of literature, painting, and music. Newman believed that the greatest contribution of the university was to cultivate a man who "can converse … can listen … can ask a question pertinently."[11]

Social Purposes of Education

Education provides the environment needed to frame and influence the mental and moral minds of the students. The purpose of school education, as John Dewey famously said, is to "ensure the continuance of education by organizing the powers that insure growth. The inclination to learn from life itself and to make the conditions of life such that all will learn in the process of living in the finest product of schooling."[12]

John Dewey's educational philosophy focused on creating the right environment for students to realize their potential by learning how to think about self and society to encourage greater accommodation and compromise. He spoke of the need to train a child to adapt to any set

---

[10] Newman, "*The Idea of a University.*"
[11] Quoted in Aoun, "*Robot-Proof,*" p. 7.
[12] Dewey, "*Democracy and Education,*" p. 31.

of conditions. "With the advent of democracy and modern industrial conditions, it is impossible to foretell just what civilization will be twenty years from now. Hence it is impossible to prepare the child for any precise set of conditions. To prepare him for the future means to give him command of himself; it means so to train him that he will have the full and ready use of all his capacities."[13] Liberal knowledge or liberal education is seen as appropriate to equip students with broad knowledge from various disciplines and develops students' ability to collect, organize, and analyze facts and opinions.

Economists advocate another moral basis of education. They coin the term "externality" to denote the impact of an individual's decision on society, which the market fails to consider. The education sector, as economists put it, exhibits strong spillovers. Jeffrey Sachs has said, "I want you to be well educated so that you do not easily fall under the sway of a demagogue who would be harmful to me as well as you."[14] Education transforms unskilled into skilled labor thereby contributing to the economic progress of a country. But some individuals may forgo the opportunity to gain a higher level of education because they are unable to factor in the full benefits of education.

The Father of Economics, Adam Smith, has called for the provision of *public* education especially for the common people "who have little time to spare for education for the benefits of the whole society."[15] The public can "facilitate," "encourage," and even "impose almost the whole body of the people" to acquire the essential parts of education.[16] Smith saw education as a tool to help bridge the gap between the classes and to achieve greater equality and stability. Smith believed that education offers the key to cultivating sympathy and the ability to understand the learning about others, accumulating knowledge, and challenging social conclusions that they may disagree with. To Smith, education provides the foundation for a decent society to produce good citizens, and so it was the responsibility of the state.

---

[13] Dewey, "*My Pedagogic Creed*," p. 6.
[14] Sachs, "*The End of Poverty*," p. 253.
[15] Smith, "*The Wealth of Nations*," p. 842.
[16] Ibid., p. 843.

The Gilded Age, from the 1870s to the early 20th century, saw the emergence of big companies that dominated various sectors and even the entire economy. Tycoons such as Cornelius Vanderbilt, John D. Rockefeller, Andrew Carnegie, and John Pierpont Morgan in the United States drove the economic expansion and became "robber barons," accumulating fame, fortune, and economic power. Pragmatic students were desperate to follow in their footsteps, to become richer and escape from unemployment and poverty, and were less interested in pursuing education to become philosopher kings, protect their liberties, and maintain social order. They wanted education to help them deal with uncertainty in a world to provide jobs, wealth, and other economic gains.

Economic Purposes of Education

The expansion of material goods and services made it necessary for individuals to seek opportunities, get a job, and earn a decent living. The purpose of education accordingly shifted to preparing the young for economic success in life, through the acquisition of knowledge and skills that are relevant to the economy and the industry. The economic calling to support industrialization, production, and consumption led to an increase in the demand for workers with practical skills. The idea of pursuing knowledge for its sake was less socially acceptable.

In 1862, United States Congress passed the Morrill Act to create land-grant universities that offered courses in agriculture and mechanical arts. Education curriculum altered its trajectory from the arts and humanities to more practical subjects to prepare students for the job market. Some of the public universities began offering courses in engineering, sciences, business administration, and teacher training.[17] Booker Washington, an influential black figure, wrote the following in 1903, which captured the essence of the issue succinctly: "There were young men educated in foreign tongues, but few in carpentry or mechanical or architectural drawing. Many were trained in Latin, but few as engineers and blacksmiths. Too

---

[17] But inclusivity was glaringly absent. The barriers imposed on the blacks in the United States had prevented them from contributing sufficiently in the markers to join the American society as equals.

many were taken from the farmer and educated, but educated in everything but farming."[18] The idea of the university was to get a degree and a good job. Essentially, the question was: How relevant is Chemistry to a bartender? How relevant is the farmer to read classics and quote from Shakespeare?

Education institutions began to design standardized curriculum and ways to teach and test. Schools looked into the factory system to create batches of students grouped by grade level and taught the same subjects in the same way and at the same pace to have workers with the right education to function in the factories and offices. Americans considered innovators like Thomas Edison and Benjamin Franklin as men of intelligence—practical men who valued common sense over abstract concepts, hands-on learning over rote memorization, and longed for education that could equip them with skills and knowledge to fix practical problems. Education was depicted as central to economic progress; the prerequisite for white-collar employment and a means to climb the economic ladder.

But there were critics such as W.E.B. Du Bois who warned against overemphasizing jobs and pursuit of dollars. They were not against the idea of the purpose of higher education as a tool to improve the standard of living of individuals. But they also favored an education system that provides for research and development and liberal arts education for consideration of a deeper knowledge of the world. The proposal gained currency and attracted support from administrators of the prominent universities.

The person most responsible for this kind of education system was Charles Elliot who served as the President of Harvard University in 1869. Eliot and later on Presidents of the Ivy Leagues believed that undergraduate education should be directed toward liberal arts to impart students with general intellectual capacities. Students could acquire professional credentials and the necessary vocational training by enrolling in specialized postgraduate education. Seeking to make university education more relevant to the nation's scientific and professional needs, Eliot expanded

---

[18] Washington, *Industrial Education for the Negro.*

the curriculum to include new programs in business, law, engineering, and medicine.

Universities in the United States consisted of many more departments and institutes; vast research libraries; a large number of people employed (administrators especially) in more locations; and expensive equipment, faculty clubs, and coffee houses, devoting to the pursuit of knowledge and producing more specialists through professional and postgraduate studies.[19] Research became more important in the United States than before, building on the successful model popularized by William Humbolt in Germany. The university would serve as a place to instruct students and further the work of the inquiry. Instructors and professors were granted freedom of expression and unrestricted communication of results and judgment. Indeed, higher education was a major channel through which the United States became a superpower.

The Rise of Technology and Digitization

We are in the midst of another significant global transition. The creation of the Internet and smartphones has created ample opportunities for new businesses and industries to emerge. At the same time, advancements in technology have created a complex and sophisticated environment that poses new demands on education.

Training enough workers with knowledge and skills to function in the offices and factories makes sense in the Industrial Age. But what should university education look like in the world exploded with (digital) technology and a universe of information that could be located at a much lower cost than before?

Contemporary thinkers of education and its role have focused their attention on moving from a single discipline solution to broad-based education. The purpose of education, according to the proponents, is to prepare the young for life beyond the university, and not just about preparing them for a particular job or profession. Education is about imparting students with soft skills and fostering greater tolerance in them to work and live with a wide variety of people.

---

[19] Kerr, "*The Uses of the University.*"

The key important issues in today's world—climate change, technological advancement, and security—are inextricably linked to education. In his book *Enlightenment Now*, renowned philosopher Steven Pinker talks about how knowledge and education can improve health and extend life (e.g., with knowledge about sanitation, safe sex, and nutrition), promote peace, democracy, and social harmony (e.g., by appreciating cultural differences and the simple fact that others could know things that we do not know, as well as appreciating that they are ways to resolve conflicts and disagreements without violence).[20] Students who enter the labor market today will encounter problems of great complexity. To computer scientists and engineers, learning beyond the sciences is an important part of our lives. The humanistic core of a liberal arts education equips students with the ability to view the world, our societies, and ourselves through disciplined reasoning, interpret new facts, appreciate their significance and impact on society, and adapt to a constantly changing environment.

In this regard, liberal or general education can serve as a useful tool to equip citizens with the ability to understand issues that are taking place nationally and globally and exert pressure to change the status quo, if necessary. Liberal education empowers the society by enabling the rightful residents to analyze and critically evaluate the actions and policies of policy makers and the government of the day so that nation states can flourish and evolve, and regimes can garner support or be replaced if they fail to deliver.

There is a network of respectable universities that consider liberal arts as essential education for students. For example, Jesuit education institutions adopt the humanitarian tradition with theology (religion), philosophy, history, and language as core part of the curriculum and with a particular focus on cultivating a person as a whole to serve the Church and the society.[21] Analyzing a sample of the core curricula in 2015 at

---

[20] Pinker, "*Enlightened Now*," p. 235.

[21] The Society of Jesus, commonly known as the Jesuits, founded the Roman College in 1551 to spread the Gospel and prepare future leaders to serve the common good. The society was founded by Ignatius Loyola in 1540. The oldest Jesuit education institution in the United States is Georgetown University in Washington, DC, founded in 1789.

nine Jesuit institutions in the United States—three universities in eastern United States (Boston College, Loyola University Maryland, and Georgetown), three universities in the Heartland-Delta region (Marquette, St. Louis University, and Loyola of New Orleans), and three universities in the west (Regis, Gonzaga, and the University of San Francisco)—Jeffrey LaBelle and Daniel Kendal concluded that (1) all the institutions require students to take courses in theology/religious studies and philosophy; (2) the institutions consider writing, literature (usually English), and history as important elements in the core; and (3) social sciences and lab-oriented sciences as well as mathematics are also important.[22] The religious and philosophical requirements show a certain uniqueness to Jesuit studies thereby reflecting the values central to Jesuit identity and presence. The primary concern is to ensure that students take courses that will strengthen their understanding of the world around them. A Jesuit higher education is not just about learning the facts of global challenges but a moral education to develop critical thinkers and self-reflective individuals and to provide experiences, activities, and courses that reflect a commitment to diversity and inclusiveness.

Arguing for liberal education, Fareed Zakaria points to the case of Facebook founder Mark Zuckerberg, a classic liberal arts and psychology major student.[23] Zuckerberg understood the interplay between technology and human psychology and broke the human barrier on the Internet where people avoided being identified by creating the culture of real identities where real people voluntarily exposed themselves to their friends. A concern with today's education is that certain nations have an overwhelming thrust for economic growth with an education system that is increasingly market oriented while putting less emphasis on skills that are useful to the students and the society.[24] Martha Nussbaum made this

---

[22] See LaBelle, J. and Jendall, D. *"Characteristics of Jesuit Colleges and Universities in the United States,"* p. 16.

[23] Zakaria, *"In Defence of a Liberal Education,"* pp. 82–83.

[24] In the quest for economic growth and development, humanities and the arts have taken a backseat. In Singapore, for example, the study of science, engineering, and technology with a skill-based curriculum received greater attention from the People's Action Party following independence in 1965 to prepare its people

point in her book *Not for Profit: Why Democracy Needs the Humanities*. Nussbaum argues that liberal education is needed to "stimulate students to think and argue for themselves, rather than defer to tradition and authority ... the ability to argue in this Socratic way is, as Socrates proclaimed, valuable for democracy."[25] Liberal education with a set of courses in philosophy, history, arts, theatre, literature, and others in the humanities is needed to prepare citizens for meaningful lives. Literature, for example, strengthens individual emotional and imaginative resources to understand both self and others whereas the use of arts that gain through music, theatre, dance, and painting cultivates sympathy by asking students to take up unfamiliar postures of thought and imagination. At the same time, courses in humanities enable the individuals to participate actively and constructively about critical issues and eventually exercise their voting rights to vote for the right person as their representatives.

Frank Ferudi sees the relevance of history and literature. He considers education as a transaction between generations. "Through education, adult society attempt to introduce children to the world as it is and provide them with the knowledge through which they can understand it."[26] As Hannah Arendt reminded us, education is about acquainting the young to the past. "Since the world is old, always older than they, learning inevitably turns towards the past, no matter how much living will spend itself in the present."[27] Academic subjects like history and literature equip students with skills that are necessary for learning and engaging with the questions and challenges thrown up by everyday life. Furedi writes, "While history or literature do not provide tips on healthy eating, they help young people to gain ideas about their place in the world and their

---

for the job market. The study of history was largely ignored. As Historian Tan Tai Yong put it "The immediate needs (following independence in 1965) were to establish the state and government, stabilize the economy, ensure social harmony, and survive challenges to its independence in a tough neighbourhood. There was no time to mull over the past or worry about recording the present for the future. History could not contribute to the priority of nation-building and economic growth." See Tan, "*The Idea of Singapore*," p. 5.

[25] Nussbaum, "*Not for Profit*," p. 48.
[26] Furedi, "*Wasted*," p. 46.
[27] Arendt, "*Between Past and Future*," p. 192.

responsibilities towards fellow human beings. The acquisition of academic knowledge provides children with a capacity to make responsible decisions … the knowledge of the past does not have a limited shelf-life."[28]

Michael Roth, who was the President of Wesleyan University, holds that liberal education is essential to create "a nation of thinking man" and "a man of action."[29] A thinking man can deal with complexity. He would reflect on the past to push forward and act independently with confidence. Higher education institutions, in Roth's view, should get away from pushing information to students. Instead, educators should encourage students to think critically through activities outside of the classroom and open-ended assessment tasks. One can imagine the importance of critical thinking and independent thinking in a society dominated by social media content. While social media has given voice to the people, the matters under discussion can be confusing and overwhelming. It is useful for the citizens to possess a wide perspective of knowledge, which higher education institutions can offer to their students, to protect them from misinformation and cyber propaganda and enable students to share and contribute their views meaningfully and convincingly.

Key proponents of liberal arts education have at least one thing in common. They studied liberal arts and continued to engage actively in one form or another in the fields of social sciences and humanities. Fareed Zakaria obtained his BA degree from Yale University and a doctorate in political science from Harvard University. He is the host of a talk show for *CNN Worldwide* and a columnist for *The Washington Post*, writing on domestic and global events and political affairs. Martha Nussbaum received her BA from New York University and her MA and PhD from Harvard University. She teaches history, philosophy, and law at the University of Chicago and is a Distinguished Service Professor of Law and Ethics at the university's Department of Philosophy. Michael Roth is a Professor in history and humanities and has taught history, literature, and philosophy. He obtained his doctorate in history at Princeton University.

Scientists and innovators are also enthusiastic about liberal arts education. Albert Einstein famously said, "The value of an education in a

---

[28] Furedi, "*Wasted*," p. 150.
[29] Roth, "*Beyond the University.*"

liberal arts college is not the learning of many facts but the training of the mind to think something that cannot be learned from textbooks."[30] Walter Isaacson who studied and interviewed innovators—people who created the Internet and computers—concluded that the humanities and the arts could provide the ingredients of human creativity such as values, intentions, esthetic judgments, emotions personal consciousness, and a moral sense, which explained why arts and humanities were valuable in science and technology. Isaacson reminded us of the story Steve Jobs told his audience during a product launch: Jobs said "It's in Apple DNA that technology alone is not enough—that it's technology married with liberal arts, married with the humanities, that yields us the results that make our heart sing." Isaacson made a crucial point that the reverse should also be true—a person who loves the arts and humanities should appreciate science and technology. Otherwise, Isaacson wrote, "they will be left as bystanders at the intersection of arts and science, where most digital-age creativity will occur."[31]

A common view among scientists is that they practice the scientific method in the confines of the ivory tower. They place great emphasis on implicit theory as a tool to explain their scientific work, almost single-handedly focus on scientific discovery while paying less attention to the realities of the world around them and leaving the effects to everyone else. This is wrong. Scientists have a moral obligation to engage with the general public and to advise and assess the effect of the scientific discovery for the simple reason that science generates tangible outcomes and affects the life of every person and species on earth. The consequence of scientific discovery can be dire. Scientists should therefore be taught the value of communicating their findings to the public and policy makers. Students of engineering and sciences should include elements of arts and humanities into their portfolio of courses to read.

The future of work will require individuals to possess high-order capacities and the ability to adapt. Looking ahead a career-minded individual will need to be almost indefinitely adaptable to fulfill the job requirements on their own with or without supervision. The new

---

[30] College of St. Scholastica, "*Is A Liberal Education Still Relevant?*"
[31] Isaacson, "*The Innovators,*" pp. 486–487.

education calls for interdisciplinary studies involving more academic fields, perhaps best described by the acronym STEAM. Nigel Cameron puts this across succinctly when he says: "The acronym STEAM, adding 'Arts' to the mix, offers a much more realistic notion of the skills needed as we move forward. Engaging with technology will be crucial, perhaps mediating between technology and its users, but human creativity and empathy will be centered to careers in a work environment dominated by Machine Intelligence."[32]

Higher Education in the Postpandemic World

Higher education has not been disrupted for centuries. Technological progress, ranging from the printing press to the invention of the radio, television, and computers, did not displace education. In many educational institutions, students are still taught the same way as to how others were taught hundreds of years ago. During these times, universities have built infrastructures such as buildings, parking services, administrative support, and residential areas that consume resources and have a high fixed cost.

With the outbreak of the coronavirus, there is an explosion of remote learning. Distance shrinks with the medium, and many believe that remote learning will be the new normal in terms of how classes will be conducted in the postpandemic world. For subjects with large enrolment, it makes sense to move them online. For example, for a class of 400 students attending lectures in a large auditorium can lend itself very well to online education. But with online learning, fewer students will be on campus. Because university facilities are not scalable, there are potentially large losses. Universities that can counter the challenge better are those that have in place systems that are more resilient and adaptable.

What should the universities do when remote learning is more widely available and acceptable? To answer this question, we need to establish three premises.

---

[32] Cameron, "*Will Robots Take Your Job?*" p. 103.

First, with machines and technology, the demand for routine knowledge work decreases. This is taking place in backend offices and in the manufacturing sector where machines are deployed to perform the work.

Second, there will an increase in the demand for nonroutine knowledge work; persons who can design solutions to solve problems. There is always work for this group of people because there is no limit to the problems that the world faces.

Third, and this is important, university education remains relevant in the digital age. The proliferation of digital tools like Google and Yahoo will not replace schools. They are complements for humans, not substitutes. Like Google and Yahoo, schools are filters. Filters work by removing what needs to be removed. They do not delete information. Good filters come in three forms. First, good filters use algorithms to run through the choices that others have made, rank them, and present the readers (students) with the top results. Google and Yahoo work this way. Second, good filters apply machine-learning systems to get to know the readers' preferences and priorities and filter the information accordingly to suit the needs of the readers so that they get what they want. That is how Amazon and YouTube work. Third, good filters know a lot of stuff and tell the readers what they need to know. That is how schools work. Google, Amazon, and others are complements for schools, not substitutes as far as filtering information is concerned. We need the three types of filters; smart algorithms to show us what we are looking for, smart machines that understand our needs and narrow the choices for us as we search for information, and smart people to interact with us to help us decipher and digest the information that we are getting from various sources. We need the filters because we do not always know what we want.

Hiring companies will not hire students because of what they know. Google or perhaps other platforms are certainly more factually knowledgeable than anyone of us. Hiring companies will hire persons who can make use of the knowledge to solve problems. The traditional way of learning where the educator stands in front of the class, delivering a lecture and trying to transfer his or her knowledge into the students' minds, is passive and not the best way of learning. Knowledge is still important. You cannot exert a good solution with an empty reservoir. But students can acquire the same information, perhaps more, by listening to even better educators through videos that available on the Internet. A new setup is needed, one that encourages students to apply the knowledge to solve problems with the educators facilitating the sessions, working with the students engagingly. Many of the most challenging problems humans face are inductive problems—problems where the right answers cannot be readily identified. We have to rely on a myriad of factors—knowledge and evidence—and make a guess based on the situation, our habits, and emotional intelligence. It is about problem solving to a large extent, thinking about solutions to problems, or even reframing the problems to move away from the mindset that there is one right answer. Universities provide a safe environment for students to explore options, try out new ideas, review the outcome measurements, and take corrective actions to rectify any deviation from the goals set.

Going to the university should not focus exclusively on getting a degree but an opportunity to acquire microcredentials—a certification in the form of badges or others to indicate competency in a specific skill. Increasingly, companies are looking for candidates to perform specific tasks for limited periods. This implies that education should put greater emphasis on general competencies that can be applied across a wide range of careers and jobs, including emotional intelligence, communication skills, self-awareness, curiosity, and self-confidence. With opportunities to work increase particularly for those with the right skills, there is an incentive for students to join the labor market even before graduation. The opportunity arises partly because of placements or internship arrangements between the university and hiring companies. Working and schooling occur at the same time; switching from work and study depends on the opportunity. University has to work with businesses, extend learning support, and candidature period to students as learning will not be confined to institutions of higher learning. The transition to a new model of teaching and learning requires time and effort. But with the lockdowns, administrators and faculty have the time to rethink the model of learning to prepare themselves as they confront the post pandemic educational environment. And they need to move fast. The credential of higher education qualifications is weakening.

CHAPTER 2

Credentials of Higher Education Qualifications

Who could be against higher education? Higher education has contributed greatly to nation building and technological progress. For some countries, higher education is a revenue-generating and export industry. For the individuals, it has helped them get into high-wage jobs and move into the middle-income class. Why does higher education need a defense?

It seems that something has happened that sort of erodes trust in higher education institutions. Parents hope that their children will find a good job. But good grades are so easy to come by that they are rendered not very useful in assessing the suitability of candidates in the hiring process. Indeed, companies are basing their hiring decisions on noneducational credentials. Coupled with rising tuition fees, the rate of return on education has declined and there is a greater unwillingness by anyone to pay more than they do now.

In the last three decades, new technologies, globalization, and off-shoring activities have transformed the world of work. Higher education is a good thing to improve workers with certain soft skills, such as showing up on time, listening carefully, and working in teams. But what else can higher education offer? What is the point of getting a degree if the education qualification is not necessary to get a job or if graduates do not have jobs that commensurate with their skills and knowledge? Students who have to borrow to finance their university education are hit with a double blow.

The notion that attainment of academic qualification does not automatically lead to higher payoff, especially for qualifications that are not entirely helpful in one's career, has been elevated as the hard truth of today's complex and competitive society. Google does not hire people because of their educational credentials. What Google looks out for is the candidate's "learning ability."[1] Salim Ismail, founding executive director of Singularity University, told Andres Oppenheimer that this is happening elsewhere. Hiring companies in start-ups prefer to rely on the individuals rating on GitHub, a cloud-based platform for programmers to post their projects and gather feedback from peers. "The value of a college degree has fallen to zero because start-ups are much more interested in a 100 rating on GitHub than a programming degree from even one of the most prestigious universities in the world … Today, your rating in GitHub is worth more than a college degree."[2] Ken Robinson and Luo Aronica reported that over 70 million young people in the world (or 13 percent of the young population aged between 15 and 24) were unemployed, and many of them were college graduates. "One reason is that there now many college graduates looking for work. The value of degrees has fallen as more and more people have them. Put simply, the currency has inflated."[3] Some of the unemployed have opted for vocational education in schools to fill jobs that require specific skills.

More people are convinced that a university education will not prepare them for work later in life. The knowledge students acquired in school will not matter because most of the things they learned in school would become obsolete by the time they graduate. More iGen'ers, writes Jean Twenge, "find no joy in school and more are cynical about its importance. School and college are now a means to an end—and high school students aren't even sure if it is the right mean anymore."[4]

Peter Thiel, the founder of PayPal, is among many others who feel that university education today is overpriced and wasting the time and energy of teens. Students enroll in the program either by force (by their parents) or with little background knowledge of what the program can do for them. As a result, they end up with the degree they do not want, and they are in debt. In March 2011, Theil announced his plan to award talented teenagers up to U.S. $100,000 each over two years to start a company

---

[1] Friedman, "*How to Get a Job at Google.*" Others like Apple and IBM have shifted their focus from recruiting candidates with degrees to those with relevant skills.
[2] Oppenheimer, "*The Robots Are Coming*," p. 257.
[3] Robinson and Aronica, "*You, Your Child and School*," p. 102.
[4] Twenge, J. "*iGen*," p. 172.

and pursue their interests with a condition that they have dropped out of college.

If higher education is worth pursuing only to do one thing, to provide the necessary training to enable him or her to participate in the workforce, then higher education is failing in this regard. In their book *Capitalism in America*, Alan Greenspan and Adrian Wooldridge wrote "There is no evidence that the economy would be better served if more people went to university; about 40% of college graduates have been unable to find a job requiring a college education. America does not need more baristas with BAs."[5]

For MBAs, scholars and practitioners have expressed concern about trying to teach management to someone who has never managed. Henry Mintzberg wrote in *Managers Not MBAs*, MBA programs are "specialized training in the functions of business, not general educating in the practice of managing. Using the classroom to help develop people already practicing management is a fine idea, but pretending to create managers out of people who have never managed is a sham."[6] Mintzberg pointed out that many of the faculty members themselves lacked first-hand knowledge about business and management. Without the craft or connection with practice, what is produced from the MBAs is "rootless, impersonal, disconnected managing."[7] Indeed, if the search for applied knowledge is the prime objective of education, any form of education especially at the postgraduate level that failed to acquire knowledge through and for practice is worse than no education at all.

Weakening of Credentials of University Education

The drive for commercial objectives is partly responsible for the weakening of the credentials of university education. Leading the pack are the diploma mills. Diploma mills are organizations that award degrees without requiring students to meet educational requirements for entry or meet educational standards for such degrees (in a typical diploma mill,

---

[5] Greenspan and Wooldridge, "*Capitalism in America*," p. 402.
[6] Mintzberg, "*Managers Not MBAs*," p. 5.
[7] Ibid., p. 94.

there are no classrooms and faculty members are often untrained, nonexistent, and unqualified). The authority to grant degrees does not come from a generally accepted independent entity, almost always a government agency. They use typical marketing methods such as telemarketing, print advertisement, and Internet tools such as e-mail, banners, and pop-ups to recruit students.

How big is the diploma mill industry? According to FBI agents Allen Ezell and John Bear, there were more than 3,300 unrecognized universities worldwide, selling bachelor's, master's, doctorates, law, and medical degrees; one international diploma mill with offices in Europe and the Middle East has sold more than 450,000 degrees; the number of fake PhDs bought each year has exceeded 50,000 out of 40,000 to 45,000 legitimate PhD degrees awarded in the United States, implying that more than half of the PhD holders have a fake degree.[8] The good news is that governments are passing laws to address the problem. Hiring companies are also taking actions against those who apply for jobs using fake qualifications and qualifications from diploma mills, resulting in loss of job, loss of professional license, deportation, and criminal prosecution. But the proliferation of diploma mills has tarnished the reputation of the higher education industry.

Then there is a proliferation of for-profit private education institutions. For-profit private schools receive no public funding and rely almost exclusively on school fees to finance their expenditures. For-profit education institutions have been criticized for ignoring strict academic standards in terms of assessment and attendance,[9] recruiting academic staff with marginal qualifications to save costs and pegging the curricula to the minimal standards.[10] Opponents to the education providers have pointed

---

[8] Ezell and Bear, "*Degree Mills*," p. 11.
[9] See Harman, "*Australian Academics and Prospective Academics*"; Marks, "*The Unsettled Meaning of Undergraduate Education in a Competitive Higher Education Environment*"; Ward, "*Academic Values, Institutional Management, and Public Policies*"; Lechuga, "*Assessment, Knowledge, and Customer Service: Contextualizing Faculty Work at For-Profit Colleges and Universities*"; Bryman, "*Effective Leadership in Higher Education.*"
[10] See Bernasconi, "*The Profit Motive in Higher Education.*"

to the lack of academic integrity, for example, by maximizing class size thereby creating a nonconducive environment for learning.[11] The curricula are dumbed down, and faculty members are pressured to pass all their students. Others have raised concerns about the role of Academic Deans of for-profit education providers who are often held responsible for meeting the financial targets of the education institutions.[12]

Corporate scandals involving for-profit schools are not uncommon. In the United Kingdom, the West London Vocational Training Centre, a for-profit college in Wales, was suspended in November 2015. It was alleged that the college has accepted fake certificates from students and used them to apply for Welsh government-funded student finance loans and grants. Students were effectively told that they could receive cash without having to attend classes regularly. The Welsh government suspended payments to the college and its students. The misconduct was exposed by a reporter posing as a potential student.[13]

Diploma mills and for-private private education institutions are not the only ones that are driven by commercial needs. Public education institutions are increasingly driven by market forces. This is mainly due to the reduction in public funding and more competition for students, which demands financial capital for the universities to improve their facilities and recruit star professors as a mean to retain and attract students.[14]

---

[11] See Kinser, "*The Quality-Profit Assumption.*"
[12] See De Boer and Goedegebuure, "*The Changing Nature of the Academic Deanship*"; Montez, Wolverton, and Gmelch, "*The Roles and Challenges of Deans.*" Academic Deans are also held responsible for safeguarding the academic rigor and standard of the courses, which makes their job particularly challenging.
[13] BBC News, "*College Payments Halted Amid Fraud Allegations*"; BBC News, "*Police Talking to Welch Government Over College Fraud.*"
[14] The drive for market efficiency has translated into extensive collaboration with private corporations, involving industries like energy and tobacco, and large companies and institutions like Enron, University of Chicago, and Princeton University. Commercial forces and corporate funding in universities has resulted in several problems, including delay in publications of research output, less sharing of academic research, manipulation of research findings to serve the commercial interest, and pouring of money into commercially promising courses such as computer science and biotechnology and scaling back on humanities. See Washburn, "*University, Inc.*"

A concern with commercial orientation is that the interest of students can be placed above everything else. Students are rewarded with a diploma or a degree without demonstrating the capability of solving challenging problems. In extreme cases, students receive the qualification without submitting an assignment or attending any class. They simply paid for the qualification. Students see going to a university as a financial transaction where they exchange cash for university education.

Because the duration of the program is significantly long (typically, an undergraduate program takes three years to complete), education providers are willing to take risks to enroll the students into the programs. If this works, the managers and administrators will receive higher compensation. The shareholders will benefit as well. If the strategies fail, the cost will be borne by the students. Students are stuck with the education institution to avoid withdrawal penalty and transfers to other schools. If the school closes down as a result of improper practice, the students lose more.

Nobel Laureate Friedrich Hayek had argued that the market would be able to make use of knowledge available to the buyers so that they could make decisions to maximize their interest. Government intervention and regulation would not be required.[15] The case of education is quite different. Participants in the education market are involved in exchanges that are not frequent or repetitive. Once enrolled, the students are "with the school" for many years, depending on the duration of the program. Being a service industry, it is also difficult for the students and parents to know the true value or genuine value of the transaction until the product is used, that is when the students are enrolled and begin to attend classes. The education providers know better than the students regarding the true learning experience and may not reveal all information, resulting in the students buying "lemons"—George Akerlof's terminology of a bad deal.[16]

The strong focus on the commercial aspect of education has led to grade inflation. When enrolling in an educational institution is seen as a financial transaction, students want to get their money's worth and turn aggressive when they are given a low grade. Indeed, students' grades have

---

[15] Hayek, "*The Use of Knowledge in Society.*"
[16] Akerlof, "*The Market for Lemons.*"

become higher and higher. In the United States, the mean GPA for both private and public schools in the 1930s was 2.3 or a C+. In 2015, it was reported that the average GPA at private universities has raised to 3.3 or a B+, whereas the average GPA at public colleges has increased to 3.0 or a B.[17] A passing grade has become a statement from the lecturer that the student has done poorly in the module instead of the usual or expected "F" grade.

Remarkably, a large number of students seem to be getting above-average good grades despite the thorough process of paper setting, double (blind) marking, rereading of scrips, use of external examiners, and others. The irony is that better grades and a higher proportion of students getting good grades do not mean that students are getting brighter and smarter.[18] Students select courses taught by teachers who are lenient graders; they often learn less along the way. The ease for students to share information about the professors through social media platforms has forced some of the professors to mark students' assignments leniently for fear of receiving poor course evaluation results from students and being labelled as harsh graders.[19] Scholars who have studied teaching evaluation have concluded that there exists a positive relationship between average grade scores and evaluation results from students.[20] With grade inflation,

---

[17] Katsikas, "*Same Performance, Better Grades.*"

[18] Stuart Rojstaczer of Duke University and his colleagues have documented the sharp increase in grade point average scores, rejecting the explanation that the increase in grades is a result of improved student quality and seeing the phenomenon more as a result of the emergence of a student as a consumer education mentality and declining academic rigour and standards. See Arenson, "*Is It Grade Inflation, Or Are Students Just Smarter?*"

[19] It is said that students come to regard their professors as service providers in the same league as a cashier in supermarkets and waiters in restaurants. They expect convenience (ease of passing the subjects with the least amount of effort and graduate in the shortest time possible) and entertainment (view their professors as performers, expecting to be engaged, persuaded, and entertained). Teachers and principals are partly to blame for the deterioration in students' behaviour in schools. To please their students, some of the faculty members avoid teaching difficult concepts and assign only a minimal number of readings.

[20] See Johnson, "*Grade Inflation.*"

the grading scheme has lost its meaning. Universities do not completely trust the grade received by students in high schools and seek to independently assess students' performance and competency. Degree classification such as firsts, upper seconds, and lower seconds can no longer be sufficiently informative.

If good grades can be easily attained, students do not feel the need to study hard. Students choose not to read the assigned readings for the subjects. They browse through the notes and review to write the term papers or prepare for the quizzes and examinations, a day or two before the due date. Students do not feel embarrassed for not doing the readings. They rarely approach the tutor for academic counselling and participate in discussions in tutorials. Many would just sit quietly in class.

Universities and colleges have become party schools, as Craig Brandon documented in his book *The Five-Year Party*. University administrators' fear of losing students to their competitors has too often turned a blind eye on students who refused to read textbooks, who did not meet the attendance requirements, and who missed class quizzes, so that they could continue to stay with the universities and colleges as paying students. When students were able to pass the subjects and obtain respectable CGPA scores with minimal effort, they used their spare time to pursue other interests—drinking and partying.[21]

Drinking and partying during the term of study is not uncommon in colleges. They begin typically on Thursday night and continues on Friday and Saturday. In some colleges, Friday classes have been removed altogether. Susan Blum told us: "On most campuses, students do everything they can to avoid early classes. Even at my 10:30 class, students are always rubbing the sleep out of their eyes, and when I taught at 9:30 they straggled in practically in their pyjamas. Friday classes are shunned altogether, to the point where some schools have simply eliminated them."[22] Drinking has been prevalent in colleges for decades and not a recent phenomenon. The difference here, as Blum points out, is that "drinking

---

[21] Brandon, "*The Five-Year Party*."
[22] Blum, "*My Word! Plagiarism and College Culture*," p. 133.

has become a scheduled activity in its own right, participated in by even the best students, and perhaps a majority of undergraduates."[23]

When students are drunk and feel tired and sleepy in class, they cannot concentrate on their studies. Students resort to cheating when submitting their work to their professors for grading. Plagiarism is a serious concern and strikes many students as the only way to get the "tasks" done. Susan Blum noted that more than 75 percent of students in American colleges admitted to having cheated while 68 percent of them admitted to having cut and pasted materials from the Internet without proper citation.[24]

The result is degradation in the quality of higher education. Kevin Carey quoted a study from the U.S. Department of Education on adult literacy and found that a majority of graduates could not compare and contrast viewpoints of newspaper editorials. "Fourteen percent of college graduates scored at only the basic level of literacy; good enough to read grade schoolbooks but not much more. The results showed a sharp decline from the same exams given a decade before."[25] Richard Arum and Josipa Roksa have collected a large sample of more than 2,300 students at four-year universities in the United States. The authors found that 45 percent of students did not show any significant improvement in critical thinking, complex reasoning, and writing skills during the first two years of college, and 36 percent of students did not demonstrate any significant improvement in learning over four years of college. Students who showed improvement tended to show only modest improvement. Nearly half would write just as badly in their junior years as when they started college.[26]

These are troubling news about the kind of education our students are receiving. But certain segments of the student population do want to study hard and expect the education institutions to maintain or even raise academic rigor and standard. They want to get good grades but only if they are reflective of the quality of the work submitted for marking. But when a curriculum is dumbed down, the practice affects all in the

---

[23] Ibid., p. 134.
[24] Ibid., p. 1.
[25] Carey, "*The End of College*," p. 9.
[26] Arum and Roksa, "*Academically Adrift.*"

university. Faculty members are doing a disservice to their students by lowering the standard of education.

Implications for Higher Education

First and foremost, we need educational leaders who understand the need and have the capability to strike the right balance the power between commercial interest and student interest.[27] Once this is in order, other reforms can be carried out.

Being an educational leader is harder than it looks. They struggle to balance educational objectives and the goal to attract and retain students—whether entry requirements should be lower or higher; how the pie of financial resources will be divided between the enriching student learning experience and distributing surpluses to owners (e.g., government representatives in the case of public universities and shareholders in the case of private education institutions). The leaders' inability to appropriately weigh short-term gains and long-term interest stems from their desire for recognition from the owners. When they recognize the importance of short-term gains, they permit improper practices to take over. Their view of the future is sorely neglected. Market forces create a race to the bottom, pushing the credentials of university education to a new equilibrium and producing a terrible outcome.

The failing of higher education is a very bad thing. It is worthy of the leaders' attention. If the universities make serious attempts to protect the student's interest and the good name of education, they would err because they have deployed resources that could have been more productively used elsewhere. But if they neglect the future outlook of the higher education sector when they had the opportunity to do something, the universities would have failed forever to do something in what could well be their most important duty.

---

[27] Academic leaders in higher education include the management team, consisting of the Chief Executive Officers, Academic Deans, and Department Heads as well as Board members who are responsible for monitoring the actions of the executive managers.

Educational leaders should recognize that there exists a "narrow corridor"—a term coined by Daron Acemoglu and James Robinson.[28] For academic institutions to flourish, both market and educational forces need to be strong. In the corridor, the administrators and academics do not just compete, they cooperate to deliver what the students, employers, and society want. If the commercial interests become too powerful, we sacrifice academic rigor and standard. If they fall behind, we end up with the ivory tower situation where university education and everyday life are disconnected. This happens when universities focus on publishing scholarly and incomprehensible academic articles that are read-only by a few with minimal resemblance to the complexity of real-life situations.

We need to balance the commercial and educational objectives, keeping in check that neither gets the upper hand. We need leaders with wisdom and self-control—leaders who give more thought to the long-term future of higher education, leaders who understand the ethical foundations and commitments they depend on, and leaders who understand the current challenges in higher education and have a strong desire to move the sector toward a more equally shared distribution of the gains from the pursuance of higher education qualifications such as better opportunities for students to engage in the working environment and reasonable returns to the institutional owners. Leaders can influence the trajectory of their respective academic institutions to keep the commercial objective in check. Failure to do so would strain the whole troop in the organization and damage everything we hope higher education could achieve.

The basic premise is that a student-centric education institution should not focus on making academic studies easy for students. To complete a degree, students are expected to think, complete the assignments, read widely, write extensively, and prepare for examinations if they are to succeed. Education entails dealing with difficult concepts and solving challenging problems. What is needed is a conducive learning environment and experience. This means putting in place systems and processes that are user-friendly, ensuring the safety of students, and availability of learning support to help at-risk students (e.g., by introducing the early

---

[28] Acemoglu and Robinson, "*The Narrow Corridor*."

monitoring mechanisms to identify and help students who are weak in their studies early in the course).

Riina Koris and colleagues have studied student–customer orientation and noted that students do not see themselves as customers on issues like curriculum design and classroom behavior. However, students expect the education institution to treat them like customers in terms of communication and feedback. Student orientation needs to be informative and helpful.[29] The implication on higher education institutions is twofold. First, the necessity to separate academic services and nonacademic services and take a stand on what is the morally right thing to do. Second, universities should realize that students expect to be treated like customers in some areas, but not in all areas of educational experience. Schools trying to cater to their students' whims and wishes are doing more harm than good.

The universities need to focus on effective teaching and recruit great teachers. Students want professors who care about them, who are passionate about teaching, and who can imbue practical elements into the subjects. Instead, universities focus on recruiting star professors who are preoccupied with research and publication rather than spending more time on fulfilling their teaching responsibility. Research-focus professors (not all of them) complain about having to teach and would get the term papers graded by teaching fellows or graduate students. The key reason for focusing on research is rather a simple one. It is research and publication that pave the way for promotions. At Harvard University, as Andrew Hacker and Claudia Dreifus noted, most of the budget per student goes to researchers; for research assistance, sabbaticals, and "loads so light that much of their pay is not for teaching."[30] Students feel short changed because they do not feel the professors are here for them.[31]

---

[29] Koris and Nokelainen, "*The Student-Customer Orientation Questionnaire (SCOQ)*"; Koris, Ortenblad, Kerem, and Ojala, "*Student-Customer Orientation at a Higher Education Institution.*" For a good summary of the students as customers debate, see Guilbault, "*Students as Customers in Higher Education*"; Guilbault, "*Students as Customers in Higher Education.*"

[30] Hacker and Dreifus, "*Higher Education?*" p. 78.

[31] Ibid., p. 83.

Some universities believe that good teaching is possible only if the professors are also active in research, to reflect the most recent thinking and findings in the field. Hence, in faculty recruitment, it is required that the applicant demonstrates research and publication in peer-reviewed journals. There are at least two problems associated with this line of thinking. First, from the students' perspective, it rarely matters that the professors are research active. As Hacker and Dreifus noted, "even committed undergraduates aren't asking for what's in the latest scholarly journals."[32] Instead, good teachers, in their view, possess the skill at explaining—the ability to clarify issues and explain abstract concepts in the way that is understood by students, and are caring—to be here for students. Second, emphasis on research and publications inevitably leads to professors wanting to teach their research topic and contents in past and upcoming articles. Hacker and Dreifus showed that much of the courses in Stanford University's History Department were not devised for the students. Rather, "they made life easier for the professor who often just has to use notes from his last article or the galleys of her next book." As a consequence, "over a quarter, more likely at least a third, of all freshmen fail to return," that is, do not make it to the sophomore year.[33]

Fareed Zakaria shares a similar thought. He noted that the publish or perish mentality has led to the development of "strange college courses" in colleges and universities. Zakaria wrote:

> Research has trumped teaching in most large universities—no one gets tenure for teaching. But as important, the curriculum has also been warped to satisfy research. Professors find that it is dreary and laborious for them to teach basic courses that might be interesting and useful for students. It is much easier to offer seminars on their current research interests, no matter how small, obscure, or irrelevant the topic is to undergraduates. As knowledge becomes more specialized, the courses offered to students become more arcane. It is this impulse that produces the seemingly absurd courses one finds in some colleges today.[34]

---

[32] Ibid., p. 83.
[33] Ibid., p. 92.
[34] Zakaria, "*In Defence of a Liberal Education,*" p. 63.

Trust in education is threatened when the universities fail to fulfill their promises. Have the universities been promising too much? Well, universities assure good jobs and good pay. They diligently conduct graduate employment surveys and showcase the starting salary of recent graduates and the employment rate. But their curriculum is outdated and is not necessarily relevant to prepare their graduates for the job market. Students absorb a collection of facts to pass the exams, yet they are of limited use the moment students walk out of the classroom and enter the labor force. Universities promise to impart core competencies such as self-awareness, communication skills, and emotional skills. It is easy to make grand promises and use clever-sounding words, but it is incredibly difficult to articulate the practicality of something so elusive. At the same time, the skills are so diverse, one wonders if the professors themselves possess the competencies. Universities appeal to students to think about and deal with global challenges of today—poverty, climate change, and global pandemic. Yet universities still operate on a paradigm of compartmentalization when we need a paradigm of diverting, relationships, and multidisciplinary.

Students believe that society needs their services and attaches a high price to a university qualification. This perception creates a sense of satisfaction and demand for higher education. When students gather the facts and read that the truth is far from the ideal as portrayed by the university, they draw a negative conclusion concerning the purpose and quality of higher education. Idealism is not wrong. But when it is misaligned with reality, it feeds into discontentment.

To regain the trust, universities should ask the question—"why are my students learning this?" Why are they studying Mathematics, Geography, History, and Science if they have no intention of becoming a Mathematician, Geographer, Historian, or Scientist? Universities prescribe subjects for their students to learn but life outside of school is not divided into subjects. Life at work and in society is multidimensional and nonlinear that requires us to apply different ways of thinking to make sense of the complex problems and challenges. A truly effective education, as Craig Adams has painfully argued, is not about absorbing a collection of facts; it is about teaching us to apply an array of different ways of thinking to solve problems. As Adams put it, "Education should give us more than the knowledge that impresses at a pub quiz. It should teach us to understand that the real power of subjects is to be found in the way of thinking that defines them—because, without that, it's almost impossible to see the connection between those countless thousands of hours of lessons and the mixed and complex questions of life itself."[35]

In sum, universities are at risk of becoming irrelevant. The business model and the focus on the marketing paradigm have led some students to perceive that they are the rightful customers and equate payment of fees to conferral of the degree. Higher education qualification has become something that can be bought. Education institutions, lecturers, students, and policy makers are all responsible for the current situation, and each party has to do more to redefine the approach and meaning of education. While most of the hiring companies continue to use higher education qualifications to tell them who to shortlist and hire, they are increasingly critical about how universities are preparing students for the workforce. When good alternatives exist (such as GitHub), they will not hesitate to switch to more reliable signals. University credentials must evolve. Higher education institutions must think about how they can deliver greater value strategically and in practice.

---

[35] Adams, "*The Six Secrets of Intelligence*," pp. 224–225.

CHAPTER 3

Jobs and Technology

Concerns have been raised about the credentials of university education and whether candidates with a degree have gained sufficient skills and knowledge to perform on the job. In this chapter, we raise another concern—whether there are enough jobs for college degree holders. We consider a question that many have asked—does technology replace jobs?

How Technology Is Taking Our Jobs

Fear of automation creating massive unemployment goes far back. Notably, the term Luddites was derived in support of Ned Ludd who in 1811 East Midlands smashed a set of framing machines in anger and in fear of the uncertainty that the Industrial Revolution could bring. The Luddites viewed invention in the 19th century during the Industrial Revolution such as the spinning jenny with suspicion and today's inventions and innovations such as the World Wide Web and smartphones raise a similar level of anxiety.

Robert Shiller uses the term "labour-saving machines narrative" to depict the use of stories to express fear of labor-saving machines on jobs. In his book *Narrative Economics*, he traced the labor-saving machines narrative from centuries ago using ancient religion and philosophical sources to concerns arising from the Internet revolution.[1] Machines such as the water-powered gin and cotton gin in the cotton industry displaced farm laborers because machines could do things faster than humans. Tractors were developed to replace human labor in toiling activities. Around

---

[1] See Shiller, "*Narrative Economics*." For a shorter version labor-saving machines narrative, see Shiller, "*Narratives About Technology-Induced Job Degradation Then and Now.*"

1870, three-quarters of Americans worked the land. Today, only around 1 percent of Americans are employed in the agriculture sector.

The unemployment rate rose during the Great Depression of the 1930s. But economic downturn was not the only contributing factor to the higher unemployment rate. It was also resulted from technological progress; displacement of labor by machines. In 1933, the great economist John Maynard Keynes warned that the world was facing "technical unemployment" due to automation; the "discovery of means of economising the use of labour outrunning the pace at which we can find new uses for labour,"[2] mirroring Karl Marx's claim that technology in the Industry Revolution would lead to the displacement of the working class.[3] The labor-saving machines narrative continued into the 1950s and 1960s. In 1962, technological automation prompted President J.F. Kennedy to declare that "the major domestic challenge of the sixties was to maintain full employment at a time when automation is replacing men."[4]

A new industrial age (the Third Industrial Revolution) brought personal computing and the Internet into our homes, factories, and offices and fear to job seekers. Old style photography leader Kodak once employed 145,000 people, losing out to new entries such as Instagram, which had just 13 employees in 2012 when Facebook purchased it for U.S. $1 billion. Firms replaced human workers with cleverly programmed machines and computers that could lift and fetch items in warehouses and factories and carry out clerical work faster and more effectively than humans.

Richard Susskind and Daniel Susskind have described how technologies are beginning to displace professionals like doctors, lawyers, educators, auditors, management consultants, and architects. It is worth quoting them at length.

> Tax preparation software and automatic filing systems displace the traditional way in which tax advice is prepared. Adaptive learning software customises how and what students are taught, in a way that cannot be replicated without one-on-one tuition. Online dispute resolution systems and document assembly software often replace

---

[2] Keynes, "*Essays in Persuasion,*" pp. 358–373.
[3] See Beeson, "*Leaning by Doing,*" p. 131.
[4] Ibid., p. 131.

the need for traditional lawyers. Online diagnostic systems enable people to try to resolve their health problems before they have to see a traditional doctor. CAD or CAE software allows architects to design, and engineers to erect, buildings that would have been unimaginable or unfeasible with a set-square and a slide rule.[5]

The fear of workers being displaced by technology is shared by Bill Gates. He noted that job replacement is coming too fast to the extent the technological disruption ought to be controlled and even slowed down. "You cross the threshold of job replacement of certain activities all sort of at once. You ought to be willing to raise the tax level and even slow down the speed."[6]

Elon Musk was similarly concerned. "What to do about mass unemployment?," he asked. "This is going to be a massive social challenge. There will be fewer and fewer jobs that a robot cannot do better. These are not things that I wish will happen. These are simply things that I think probably will happen."[7]

Stephen Hawking has claimed that "the automation of factories has already decimated jobs in traditional manufacturing, and the rise of artificial intelligence is likely to extend this job destruction deep into the middle classes, with only the most caring, creative or supervisory roles remaining."[8]

Carl Benedict Frey and Michael Osborne analyzed the potential impact of contemporary technologies on jobs using data from the U.S. Department of Labor and found that 47 percent of total U.S. employment were in the high-risk category; jobs that could be automated relatively soon. A further 19 percent of jobs were in the medium-risk category. The most vulnerable workers are those in the transportation and logistics industries together with office and administrative support workers in production companies.[9]

---

[5] Susskind and Susskind, "*The Future of the Professions*," p. 113.
[6] Quote from Delaney, "*The Robot That Takes Your Job Should Pay Taxes, Says Bill Gates*."
[7] Quote from Larson, "*A Warning From Bill Gates, Elon Musk, and Stephen Hawking*."
[8] Hawking, S. "*This Is the Most Dangerous Times for Our Planet.*"
[9] Frey and Osborne, "*The Future of Employment.*"

Boyd Cohen asserted that with the growing power of technologies such as artificial intelligence and big data, economies are witnessing a "great decoupling" of productivity gains. "Until the 1980s, there was a very strong correlation between increased productivity, GDP, job and income growth. Yet, around the time the Internet emerged, we started witnessing a decoupling of these constructs. While companies may continue to reap the rewards of productivity-enhancing technologies, the middle and lower classes of society are witnessing a decline in jobs and income."[10] Advanced countries like the United States no longer hold onto their comparative advantage in producing high value-added tradable goods components. Economic activities that were once prevalent in the United States, Europe, and Japan are now dominant in developing and emerging countries like China, India, Vietnam, and elsewhere. These countries have as a result become more competitive in areas which the advanced countries used to dominate. With globalization and technological advancement, it does not matter as much where the goods are produced. Tradable goods can be produced and consumed anywhere. As a result, employment in the tradable sector in the United States barely grew between 1990 and 2008.[11] Employment in the high end of the value-added chain and nontradable part of the economy was less affected—in finance, computer design, and top management positions in multinational enterprises—which generally employed highly educated persons.

Along the spectrum of the supply chain, countries at the lower end of the economic spectrum have begun to participate in a wider range of economic activities. Countries like Cambodia and Vietnam have moved from reliance on exports of commodities and raw materials to exporting parts and components of goods and assembling of products to the industrialized nations. Technologies and capital to employ were mostly imported from abroad (such as multinational corporations), requiring

---

[10] Cohen, "*Post-Capitalist Entrepreneurship*," p. xv.
[11] Michael Spence reported that the tradable sector that accounted for more than 34 million jobs in 1990 grew by a "negligible" 600,000 jobs during this period. Spence, "*The Impact of Globalisation on Income and Employment*," p. 30. See also Fort, Pierce, and Schott, "*New Perspectives on the Decline of US Manufacturing Employment*."

more locals to upgrade their educational qualifications and skillsets. Labor costs have steadily increased in these countries. As wages start to increase, companies automate as it is more cost-effective to automate than employing and paying benefits to workers. Cohen, citing a report by the International Labour Organization, noted that up to 90 percent of the garment and footwear workers in Cambodia and Vietnam are at risk of losing their jobs as a result of factory automation.[12]

The fear of losing a job can be harmful and emotionally stressful to unemployed persons. At France Telecom, a spate of suicides and attempted suicides have been reported after the company slimmed down its management in 2007–2008. Adrian Wooldridge wrote "One man stabbed himself in the middle of a business meeting" (he survived). A woman leapt from a fifth fifth-floor window after sending a suicide e-mail to her father: "I have decided to kill myself tonight—I can't take the new reorganization."[13] According to Princeton University economist Anne Case and Angus Deaton, joblessness has led to suicidal thoughts, consumption of drugs and alcohol, and contributed to increase in deaths and shorter life expectancy. They call these "deaths of despair."[14] The discontentment with automation and industrial robots, argued Daron Acemoglu and Pascual Restrepo, has contributed to Donald Trump's victory in the 2016 Presidential Election and not the inflow of immigrant immigration as some have noted.[15] Countries such as Italy and Britain reacted by enacting laws to protect workers by slowing down digital transformation. In southern Europe, laws are introduced to make it slow, expensive, and difficult to dismiss a worker for any reason. The policy goal is to protect the workers and "ensure that workers are not the only ones to bear the cost of changes."[16] The impact of technology on employment is real and has become a sensitive issue in many countries.

Fearing of misdirected aspiration among the citizens, governments have made a deliberate effort to sway the decision from acquiring a degree

---

[12] Cohen, "*Post-Capitalist Entrepreneurship*," p. xv.
[13] Wooldridge, "*The Great Disruption*," p. 20.
[14] Case, A. and Deaton, A. "*Deaths of Despair*."
[15] Quoted from Edsall, "*Robots Can't Vote, But They Helped Elect Trump*."
[16] Quoted from Baldwin, "*The Globotics Upheaval*," p. 231.

that is not relevant to their careers. In January 2014, for example, the Ministry of Education in Singapore published the ASPIRE report, advising students and parents to think through the career options and the various training courses that are available in the market before signing up for a degree. The Ministry raised the concern that students who have invested time and money to obtain an undergraduate or postgraduate degree might not be able to land on jobs that commensurate with their newly acquired qualifications. However, the ASPIRE committee acknowledges that changing the mindset of students and parents "to go beyond qualifications, to go beyond the classroom, to go beyond narrow definition of success" is a tall order and will take many years, if at all, to make the society change.[17]

Undoubtedly, some people are concerned about the perceived ills of globalization and immigration. They are upset with declining wages, jobless growth, and a net decline in real wages. Among the workers in advanced countries, the biggest losers are those with a lower level of education. This is because of the movement of labor-intensive economic sectors such as electronic appliance assembly, apparel cutting and shoemaking to emerging and developing countries. As the prices of these globally traded goods fall, the wages of low-skilled workers in the advanced countries are also pushed down.

Some of them have responded by acquiring a degree. The notion that one does not know how the future would turn out or the kind of jobs that would emerge in the new future gives one the hope that higher education would give them an advantage. Essentially, getting a degree gives them a sense of security; more education means that they are better able to make the transition, and when they lose a job, they are in a better position to get a new job.

---

[17] See Varaprasad "*50 Years of Technical Education in Singapore*," p. 151. The 21st century is a very different world, a time when iron rice bowls hardly exist. Phillip Brown, Hugh Lauder, and David Ashton told us that there is a global auction for high-skill low-wage workers, attributed to the huge supply of university graduates especially from the emerging countries who are skilled and are willing to accept lower wages than those in their home country. Brown, Lauder, and Ashton, "*The Global Auction.*"

Often, the decision to further one's education has support from the government. The government recognizes that in a high-tech information-driven world, successful economies need more educated people to acquire the right skills and knowledge. It is not uncommon for the government to subsidize training to encourage individuals to upgrade themselves by taking relevant courses and for firms to send their staff for specific training. This forms part of the social program, popular in welfare states, to help increase the size of the labor force by encouraging and preparing more people to enter it.

As noted in Chapter 2, the trust students place in formal university education in fulfilling their goals has weakened. Many would think twice before entering university, considering other options that are available in the market. When good alternatives to university credentials exist, they would not hesitate to switch to more reliable signals to demonstrate to hiring companies their competencies and capabilities.

Humans Versus Technology: Another Viewpoint

For years, countries have expressed worry about migrants taking away jobs from the locals due to their lower wages. The worry is valid since humans can indeed replace humans. But can technology replace workers? To some extent yes—in particular, routine and heavy lifting jobs.

But in other occupations, machines are complements for humans, rather than substitutes. As Peter Theil told us, machines and humans are fundamentally good at different things. Humans can make plans and decisions in complicated situations. We assess the situations, consider options, factor in our judgment, experiences and be guided by a moral compass. But we are not so good at making sense of the enormous amount of data. Computers are exactly the opposite. They excel at data processing but they lack common sense and emotional intelligence and struggle to make the basic judgment.[18]

Some jobs require a human touch and are hard to replace. While machines can replicate logical functions of human intelligence, doing it faster and better than we can, the realm of emotional intelligence, empathy

---

[18] See Thiel (with Masters), *"Zero to One,"* p. 143.

and imagination—all necessary in the context of incomplete information or conflicting aims—is beyond the reach of the machines. Yuval Noah Hariri noted that humans have two types of abilities—physical and cognitive. While machines can perhaps do better than human in "raw physical abilities," humans "retained an immense edge over machines in cognition."[19] The cognitive skills include learning, analyzing, communicating, and understanding human emotions, which put humans at an advantage. Yoval Noah Hariri cited the example of driving a vehicle in a street full of pedestrians, negotiating a business deal, caring for the elderly which require a good motor and emotional skills that technology cannot effectively replace at least for now.

Think about the job market as consisting of three categories. At one end, there are service sector jobs involving interaction with fellow humans in an unpredictable environment such as driving a bus, cooking food and caring for the children and the elderly. The middle tier involves jobs that are white-collar and routine such as data filing, data entry and form filling, which are increasingly done by machines. Finally, at the top, some jobs require creativity, problem solving, decision making, negotiating, which are increasingly complex due partly to globalization and regulatory compliance, and would continue to be executed by humans.

Robert Gordon, an economist from Northwestern University argued that innovations in 3D printing, robots, and artificial intelligence would evolve gradually rather than suddenly result in the massive loss of jobs, allowing new markets and new jobs to emerge to minimize the impact of innovation on job losses. In the case of robots, not many of them seem to appear in retail stores, restaurants, hotels, construction sites, commercial aircraft, and hospitals. "Part of the problem with robots," Gordon told us, "is that they are not yet adept at many of the routine tasks performed by humans, including hopping off trucks to deliver packages."[20] John Browne, former Chief Executive of BP, echoed the same sentiment. In *Make, Think, Imagine: Engineering the Future of Civilization*, he wrote that although an increasing amount of the machines' output appears to be

---

[19] Harari, "*21 Lessons for the 21st Century*," p. 19.
[20] Gordon, "*Declining American Economic Growth Despite Ongoing Innovation*," p. 9.

the product of some form of "genuine intelligence," one must remember that the systems "can still only provide insights based on deductions from past events." And "everyone who worries about the arrival of supremely powerful artificial intelligent machines should consider the challenge of maintaining machines even today—the unpredictable behaviour of an office printer is a good example." While computers can outperform human intellect in many specific tasks, and engineer will continue to build and program computers that support us in many ingenious ways, "silicon-based intelligence with the same qualities as human intelligence has yet to arrive."[21]

Machines and computers receive orders of steps triggered by conditions in advance. Heuristics exists to guide and restrict actions and to decide when to give up. Machines and computers can extract texts and words from published sources. But they struggle to process natural language due to the complexity in thematic and grammatical forms. Coupled with the lack of social and emotional intelligence, machines and computers perform limited functions like searching huge collection of texts, reminding us about shopping and visits, and translating documents albeit imperfectly (readers normally ignore grammatical errors and poor word choices). They hardly understand what the words mean or grasp the meaning of what they read or say (e.g., Siri).[22] "Machines are less promising than many people assume," wrote Margaret Boden. More specifically about Artificial Intelligence (AI), she argued that there are "countless things that AI cannot do … AI has focused on intellectual rationality while ignoring social/emotional intelligence—never mind wisdom. An AI that could interact fully with our world would need those capacities too."[23]

Machine intelligence is not everything. As James Beeson told us, "Computers might diagnose better than the average doctor if they are given all the symptoms, but nurses and doctors can read body language and nonverbal cues to detect symptoms … Computers can select financial portfolios and make investment recommendations, but they might

---

[21] Browne, "*Make, Think, Imagine*," p. 43.

[22] However, things are moving quickly. By the time this book is published, there may be exceptions in terms of what machines and computers can do.

[23] Boden, "*Artificial Intelligence*," p. 136.

not provide secure guidance to investors panicking because the market is down 30 percent. Computers can compare product prices and specifications, but sales representatives also help consumers reason through which features are most important to them, and they build trust that a supplier will respond well to unforeseen contingencies."[24] The more we automate the routine staff, George Anders warned, "the more we create a constant low-level human of digital connectivity, the more we get tangled up in the vastness and blind spots of big data, the more essential it is to bring human judgment into the junctions of our digital lives."[25] In a way, computers and machines magnify the importance of humans and our cognitive ability to judge, innovate, and empathize (whether as teachers, administrators, or salespersons).

An important point to note is that humans are a unique species. Psychologists have pointed out that human behavior is influenced by the conscious and unconscious brain. The experience and actions are almost always rooted in conscious thought. But there is also the subliminal brain, which is invisible to us, yet it influences our conscious experience of the world, attaching meanings to everyday events and helping us to make quick decisions that can sometimes affect our lives. The unconscious mind distinguishes us from machines and computers. "We are not like computers," wrote Leonard Mlodinow, author of *Subliminal*. Computers "crunch data in a relatively straightforward manner and calculate results." Our brains on the other hand are made up of "a collection of many modules that work in parallel, with complex interactions, most of which operate outside of our consciousness."[26]

Mlodinow told the story of his relationship with his college, the late Stephen Hawking.[27] Mlodinow recalled that unconsciously he could

---

[24] Beeson, "*Leaning by Doing*," p. 132.
[25] George "*You Can Do Anything*," pp. 4–5.
[26] Mlodinow, "*Subliminal*," p. 22.
[27] Stephen Hawking, a well-known theoretical physicist, was diagnosed with Amyotrophic lateral sclerosis, a type of motor neurone disease. He could hardly move a muscle and had to rely on specially designed software to help him communicate and type letters and words he wanted to express on a screen. He died in March 2018 at the age of 76.

relate and understand Hawking's mood; his frustrations and happiness, "detecting when his attention shifted from the cosmos to thoughts of calling it quits and moving on to a nice curry dinner. I always knew when he was content, tired, excited, or displeased, just from a glance at his eyes." He concludes that while language is handy, "humans have social and emotional connections that transcend words, and are communicated—and understood—without conscious thought."[28] Human socialism and the ability to sense and feel is something that machines cannot replace.

Can Technology Create a Net Positive Impact on Employment?

Some have argued that while technology has replaced certain jobs, new opportunities and new jobs are being created. Look at Amazon. There was speculation that warehouse automation in Amazon would result in the loss of 15,000 jobs. Yet, in 2018, Amazon announced that it would hire 50 percent more people during the same period and announced its plan to add 100,000 new jobs.[29]

That technological progress can create opportunity and new jobs are evident from the historical perspective. Before the invention of cars, people used horses to travel from one place to another. With the introduction and expansion of the automobile industry, the livelihood of horse-cart drivers and blacksmith (reshoe horses) was threatened. But the automobile industry has also inspired new industries and new job opportunities, making room for auto-mechanics, road construction crews, driving instructors, car dealers, car washers, motor-insurance agents, traffic safety officers, parking lot attendants, map makers, and personal-injury lawyers. Similarly, the digital age has led to the demand for market researchers and marketing specialists to help companies make sense of data supported by cheap online survey and data analytical tools. Technology might have eradicated some jobs but at the same time, it has created new openings that could not have existed before. Some of the jobs are tech-influenced but not tech-centric, including compliance officers,

---

[28] Mlodinow, "*Subliminal*," p. 80.
[29] As reported in Oppenheimer, "*The Robots Are Coming!*" p. 56.

entertainment producers and directors, event planners, fundraisers, genetic counsellors, graphic designers, human resource specialists, management analysts, market research analysts, marketing specialists, school administrators, technical writers, childcare teachers, and nurses.

Paul Krugman gave the example of the hotdog business, which shows how an increase in productivity due to mechanization can lead to higher output in the company thereby creating more job opportunities for those whose jobs were displaced by machines.

Consider a hotdog restaurant with four workers: Ann, Beatrice, Cathy, and Donna. Ann works at the cashier counter.[30] Beatrice prepares the sausages. Cathy bakes the bun and Donna put the sausage and bun together. Suppose the restaurant owner has decided to go cashless and install a self-paid machine, displacing Ann as a result. Installing the machine makes economic sense as it can raise productivity and lower the cost of production. What will happen to Ann? She may underestimate the risk and choose to do nothing, believing that she can outrun the bad event and easily find a new job. Or she may want to take a pay cut to rejoin the labor force. Or she may choose to upgrade her skills, for example, by learning how to prepare the sausages. The last option can lead to a reduction in the wages for sausage-preparers, lowering Beatrice standard of living in the process. Krugman offers a fourth possibility. As a result of the increase in productivity and lower cost of production, the hotdog restaurant owner chooses the decrease the hotdog prices. The demand for hotdogs will rise, and the firm responds by producing more hotdogs than before to meet the demand. There is more work to be done. Ann, with her newly acquired skills, can find work as a sausage-preparer. There also be more jobs for bun-makers and hotdog-compilers because of the increase in the output of hotdogs. There is less of a worry about the fall in the number of employees in the firm if the new jobs that are created exceed the number of job loss and if those workers affected by technology learn new skills.

Krugman illustrates how the increase in productivity in the hotdog sector is capable of creating employment opportunity in the bun sector. Replacing hotdogs with manufacturers and replace buns with services,

---

[30] This is a modified version of a story told in Susskind and Susskind, "*The Future of the Professions,*" p. 285.

Krugman's story resembles the U.S. economy in the last three decades of the 20th century. Krugman wrote "Between 1970 and the present, the economy's output of manufactures roughly doubled; but, because of productivity increases, employment declined slightly. The production of services also roughly doubled–but there was little productivity improvement, and employment grew by 90 percent. Overall, the U.S. economy added more than 45 million jobs. So, in the real economy, as in the parable, productivity growth in one sector seems to have led to job gains in the other."[31]

The argument behind Krugman's story is that technological advancement allows firms to enjoy cost savings, which are passed on to the consumers in terms of lower prices. This leads to higher demand for the product and related goods and services, creating new jobs for the people. Technology in this regard can be both destructive, by displacing people from their job and constructive, by creating new jobs.

Kartik Gada, a renowned futurist, asserted that digitization has brought about rapid price deflation, contributing to more output from the private and public sectors. This happens because technology advancement has helped organizations to perform at lower cost than a human and as a result, technology has created more jobs that it has destroyed.[32]

The information and communication technology revolution has also permitted the separation of production and consumption over long distances in services. Firms and nations concentrate not only on things they make but also on things they do. With digital technology, the expansion of services across nations has grown from strength to strength. For example, machine translation (such as Google translation) enables foreigners to communicate in good-enough English or German and work at a fraction of the labor cost in the United States and Germany. The use of online matchmaking platforms (such as upwork.com) help companies locate and assign jobs to workers to take advantage of international wage differentials.[33]

---

[31] Krugman, "*The Accidental Theorist*."
[32] Gada, "*ATOM*."
[33] See Baldwin, "*The Globotics Upheaval*."

When we speak about the job, it is more accurate to refer to the many different tasks that form part of the job. In most cases, the job is not made up of one single task. It consists of a diverse set of tasks. If humans are no longer required to perform a certain task, it is possible that the remaining tasks are bundled to redefine the job or more work is needed to be done in other tasks, which can correspondingly lead to more job opportunity. The Automatic Teller Machines (ATMs), for example, could perform simple tasks, but they did not take over all of the tasks of bank tellers, especially those that involved human interactions such as relationship building with customers or explaining new products to potential clients. By lowering the cost of operation, ATMs have allowed banks to increase the number of branches and raised the demand for tellers to perform tasks that the ATMS could not undertake.

There is still hope for the school system, to prepare students for the world of work by equipping them with knowledge and skills that they can use for the good of the business community and the society as a whole. We know that jobs that require routine cognitive input are most at threat, so teaching skills and knowledge that can be tested and taught easily should be avoided as these skills and knowledge are the easiest to digitize and automate. To move forward, education providers have to understand and get a strong grip on the outcomes they want from the schooling system. This entails knowing what students learn in schools, the ways of working in the world of work, the tools for working and the ways of thinking that employers demand, and the assessments that can be constructively designed to achieve the stated goals and objectives. It is about carefully thinking through the expected learning outcomes of the modules and the topics covered and attributes of the graduates.

In addition, it can be argued that the economic calling to support industrialization and production and consumption in the digital age will result in an increase in the demand for workers especially those with digital skills. New occupations have emerged; data scientists, computer operators, coders and many others. With training and retraining, the displaced workers—middle-education persons in blue-collar production and operations positions as well as those white collars occupations such as clerks—can fill the new vacancies.

Educators must be aware of the potentialities that technological progress can bring; to expose individuals to new experiences and lead students into new fields of study. After all, one of the objectives of learning has to be in preparation for students to secure a job in and for the future.

With change happening so fast, one who enrolls in primary education today will have no idea the kind of jobs that will be available 10 years down the road. This is not the case for one who enrolls into the university today. There is greater certainty in terms of the types of jobs that are available and in demand. A case can be put forth therefore for the university to impart skills and knowledge that employers want, and leverage on microcredentials possibly in partnership with employers and industry associations so as to get students up to date with the required specialized and technical skills.

Educators should know that in a global economy, the need to be cost-effective will be increasingly important to stay relevant and win business. As such, all work that can be digitized and automated will be digitized and automated. What needs to be taught is an important consideration. Many institutions of higher learning make the mistake of failing to teach their students contents and skills that employers need, and how to organize and use knowledge after they acquire it.

Universities have to lead the initiative to retain their relevance. Universities should work with firms and industries to appreciate the industry requirements but they should not rely on them to help save jobs. Firms and the people who design and deploy technology are not motivated by the desire to expand human capital or create new jobs or even make existing jobs more interesting. They are motivated by the desire to make money. As Nicholas Carr told us, "jobs have always been a by-product of the market's invisible hand, not its aim."[34]

---

[34] Carr, "*Utopia Is Creepy and Other Provocations,*" p. 177.

CHAPTER 4

Staying Relevant in the Digital Age

Despite much criticisms about the relevance of higher education, people's lives continued to be transformed through university education. One reason, as Derek Bok explained is that "even work that is still performed by employees with only a high school education may be done better or more effectively by college graduates."[1] Acquisition of attributes in the university such as the ability to communicate clearly, solve unknown problems confidently and work cohesively in teams can make the students more productive than workers in the same job who have less education.

And signaling still matters to a large extent. Hiring companies use education qualification to reflect the candidate's suitability in filling a job vacancy, particularly for earlier-career candidates. The candidates lack professional working experience, hence hiring companies cannot accurately assess the potential contribution and acumen of the job applicants. Educational credentials fill the gap.[2]

Students and parents also know that technological development will not eliminate jobs straightaway. Steven Pinker puts this across this way: "Until the day when battalions of robots are inoculating children and

---

[1] Bok, *Higher Education in America*," p. 83.
[2] See Van de Meer and Wielers, "*Educational Credentials and Trust in the Labor Market*"; Verhaest and Verhofstadt, "*Overeducation and Job Satisfaction*." John List, a renowned professor of economics from the University of Chicago, tells the story of his difficulty in entering the job market following the completion of his PhD. He applied to more than 150 academic positions but was given only one interview. He later learned that the key difference between himself and other candidates was that he received his PhD from the University of Wyoming whereas the other candidates received theirs from more reputable universities like Harvard and Princeton. See Gneezy and List, "*The Why Axis*," pp. 10–11.

building schools in the developing world, or for that matter, building infrastructure and caring for the aged in ours, there will be plenty of work to be done."[3] As I have shown in Chapter 3, the impact of technological progress on jobs is inconclusive. Indeed, in the advanced countries, individuals with higher education qualification actually earned more on average while those with a lower level of education earned less. The former is employed in the higher end of the value-added chain in areas where advanced countries continue to have a comparative advantage.[4]

For these reasons, there is still a strong demand for university education. In China, for example, only 117,000 students attended colleges or universities in 1949. The number of college or university students increased to 37 million by 2015, studying in one of the 3,000 odd universities and colleges in the country.[5]

But fueled by technological progress and the reluctance (and total neglect) from higher learning institutions to catch up with the new realities, the future of education is at risk as we have argued in Chapter 2. The universities can destroy themselves and tarnish the relevance of higher education. What can they do to stay relevant in the digital age?

When technology is introduced and the output of the economy increases, a new set of tasks is created and has to be performed in addition to the existing set of tasks that have not been displaced by the technology. There are also new industries that are established which will need people with relevant skills and knowledge. These are the areas where employment opportunity would arise. The World Economic Forum has reported that firms are increasingly interested in adopting robots and artificial intelligence with cloud computing, big data and e-commerce remain high in priorities. Roles at risk of being displaced by technologies include data entry clerks, administrative and executive secretaries, accounting and bookkeeping clerks, assembly and factory workers, and business services and administrative managers. By 2025, 85 million jobs could be displaced across the 15 industries and 26 economies covered although 97 million

---

[3] Pinker, "*Enlightened Now*," p. 300.
[4] See Claudia Goldin's and Lawrence Katz's detailed study of the American education sector. Goldin and Katz, "*The Race Between Education and Technology*."
[5] Zhao, "*China Has One in Five of All College Students in the World: Report.*"

jobs might emerge. Jobs in high demand include data analysts and scientists, artificial intelligence and machine learning specialists, robotic engineers, and software and application developers.[6]

It seems to me that university education is not about teaching specific knowledge and skills for a specific job (like website tracking using Google or managing operations on Alibaba cloud). That is the role of the employers and professional associations. But universities can work with the employers and professional associations to offer short courses or incorporate subjects in partnership with the employers and professional associations into the courses that they offer. The core function of universities is to provide a holistic education, to prepare students for working life by teaching both hard and soft skills needed for the workplace, and to impart their students with the ability to teach themselves new skills on the job. It will not be about how much education that matters but what kind of education. It will be about learning things in school's that are relevant in the age of digitization and globalization.

How Can Higher Education Stay Relevant in the Digital Age?

- Offer Courses That Employers Need

If education is about job training, what really matters is the alignment of university curriculum with industry needs.

Most of us can agree that every large organization is thinking about incorporating machine learning, artificial intelligence, and digital technologies in their business operations. This means that a lot of repetitive tasks at the workplace will be automated. What organizations need more in this regard are employees who are able to perform nonrepetitive tasks and persons who can find problems as opposed to solve problems.

Universities need to prepare students to think in a more diverse and cross-functional way to successfully navigate the increasingly complex and multidimensional nature of life and work in the 21st century.

---

[6] World Economic Forum, "*The Future of Jobs Report 2020.*"

Consider the media industry. In news media, readers in the digital age can access to news at any time of the day through a variety of platforms. To stay relevant, news media outlets must focus on producing deep analysis of issues and events and original insights. These are certainly critical, but they are not sufficient. They must also tap on digital platforms and technology to push the contents to the readers. To do so, they would need to build a digital team comprising journalists, IT engineers, digital marketers, online media professionals, and graphic designers to support the design and delivery of enterprise functionality. The success of the team rests on the members' ability to combine deep skills each has in one or more fields and a high level of understanding across many others, to analyze trade-offs over the entire space of design alternatives and evaluate the quality and effectiveness of service provision that directly impact the readers.

Building cross-disciplinary collaborative teams is not uncommon nowadays in organizations and work settings to provide a multidimensional perspective in addressing a specific problem. It recognizes that making decisions is difficult because the facts are uncertain. Decisions should not be based on single evaluation judgment. Multidisciplinary consideration contributes to the overall understanding of the issues and challenges. In a team with IT and other professionals, IT professionals understand the business needs and all knowledge workers understand how IT and digital tools can affect the design, production, and delivery of services with the ultimate aim of generating greater business value to the particular needs of customers. This can be important when we deal with a dilemma. Reasons that incorporate multiple perspectives supply the input necessary to reach a responsible and intelligent decision. Indeed, anyone with an important decision to make can benefit from advice from different aspects of the problem from different people. The good news is that the capacity to view the problem simultaneously from the viewpoint of another person, and from the point of one's relations to others is unique among humans.[7]

---

[7] The danger arises when we fail to justify the multidimensional nature of the problems by willingly brush aside unexplained causes and consequences. It may be the case that the problems are difficult to solve. But unsolvable problems are

Scientists and engineers recognize that technology and scientific knowledge alone is not enough. Knowledge in liberal arts and humanities is important. Liberal arts and humanities classes nurture students' thoughts with originality and humanity, and train them to keep asking why and taking the wide views thereby "allowing them to pick up important factors on the periphery that they might otherwise overlook."[8] Students acquire the ability to find extra facts quickly, finding insights and clarity through lateral thinking, analyzing the situation and identifying hidden factors, synthesizing insights to help make complex decisions, and instilling in students an open mind confident in exploring the new (rather than following the majority). For example, English majors are good storytellers. The demand for individuals who can inform and inspire—old-fashioned communication abilities—remains strong in the digital age. Notably, universities offering STEM courses recognize that most of their students will not go on to be scientists, and hence having the intellectual tools in the humanities and social sciences can be essential for their students regardless of their future occupation.

For the arts, social sciences, and liberal arts students, appreciation of mathematics and computing is useful to avoid being left out in the age that is defined largely by the application and development of technology

---

not unreal problems. Some of the peculiarity of the working environment can be explained by obligation to serve a particular function in a rigidly defined rule. As a result, an individual may sometimes say that it is obliged to consider only his function as if it would be a breach of responsibility to consider anything else. I therefore believe that we need to extend individual obligations and commitment. Students should trust problems over solutions, cooperation versus competition and complexity over elegance and simplicity. Multidisciplinary consideration contributes to the overall understanding of the issue. In large-scale social environment, we reflect, consider the trade-offs, weight the consequences, and decide what to pursue and what to avoid given the circumstances. Perhaps unconsciously, we make decisions and support our claims based on habit and assessment that we never question, seeing ourselves from the outside. Sometimes we need team members—an outsider—to remind us of our prejudices, to see things from other perspectives to which we should appreciate to fulfill our service to the stakeholders.

[8] George, "*You Can Do Anything*," p. 41.

and digitization. The economic calling to support industrialization and production and consumption has led to an increase in the demand for workers with knowledge in science, technology, and computing. This means that students can learn different majors or acquire liberal arts education with electives, for example, in digital analysis and coding embedded into the course. Whether you are recruited as a journalist, teacher, or sales consultant, hiring companies are looking for candidates who can use various platforms such as graphic, audio, text, and video in an integrated way.

IT vendors such as IBM are already partnering education institutions to train interdisciplinary professionals. They are shifting the effort away from educating narrowly focused specialists to T-shaped professionals. T-shaped professionals possess deep skills in a particular discipline and they have sufficient understanding of a broad range of disciplines to appreciate trade-offs and participate constructively in interdisciplinary collaborative teams.

In 2013, IBM launched the Service Science, Management and Engineering (SSME) initiative, working closely with universities around the world to design and develop cross-disciplinary courses. The purpose is to educate a new generation of SSME professionals who are capable of integrating service science knowledge and skills across disciplines to address real-world problems in healthcare, water, energy, supply chain, and transportation as part of IBM's Smarter Initiative project.[9]

Universities benefit by tailoring their curriculum and research to world needs and provide students with training that cuts across disciplines. The prevalent view is that it is no longer sufficient for higher education institutions to see themselves as mere institutions that award degrees. The more important consideration is the design and development of curricula, consisting of knowledge and skills that students and employers want, to form a package of what we call a degree. Education institutions such as Carnegie Mellon, MIT, and North Carolina State in the United States have created interdepartmental curricula and research initiatives to prepare students for the future of work.

---

[9] See Lusch and Wu, "*A Service Science Perspective on Higher Education*"; Spohrer, Fodell, and Murphy, "*10 Reasons Service Science Matters to Universities.*"

In Singapore, universities are offering more dual degrees and interdisciplinary degrees. Singapore University of Technology and Design, despite its focus on technology, requires students to take subjects in humanities and social sciences. Singapore's oldest university, National University of Singapore (NUS), would bring together the Faculty of Arts and Social Sciences and Faculty of Science to form a College of Humanities and Sciences. Tan Eng Chye, President of NUS, noted that young adults today need to grapple with "wicked problems," problems that are ill-defined and multidisciplinary. As such, NUS "will ease the excessive requirements for subject majors so that we can add breath to the curriculum overall. If we want our students to be able to connect the dots in new and unusual ways, it helps to broaden their horizons and expose them to more dots."[10]

In her book *The New Education: How to Revolutionize the University to Prepare Students for a World in Flux*, Cathy Davidson wrote that "the college education we need today must prepare our students for their epic journey, the mountain and the cliff's edge. It should give them agency, arm them to take on a different world, to push back and not merely adapt to it."[11] To prepare students for this journey, students must be exposed to a range of complex skills and knowledge. Davidson told the story of Patrick Awuah who founded Ashesi University in Ghana. Awuah was educated in the United States, employed as an executive in Microsoft but decided to set up a university in his own country. Ashesi University combines a liberal arts school and a professional school and aims to prepare Ghanaians for the future. The structure of education at Ashesi University is quite dissimilar to that of the United States. In the latter, students begin with broad general education before narrowing their field of student, leading to independent studies and capstone projects. At Ashesi University, students begin with the research project, exposing them to various disciplines and curriculum and major real-world events. This way, students realize that without attending to economic, social, political, sciences, and cultural conditions, they would achieve very little. Students learn that sciences and technology alone or any specific discipline for that matter is not enough to address actual life issues. In subsequent

---

[10] Tan, "*Universities Need to Tear Down Subject Silos*."
[11] Davidson, "*The New Education*," p. 13.

terms of study, students in Ashesi University read a wide range of texts in history, philosophy, and others to learn about different viewpoints and acquire the skill to interpret and analyze information critically. "Writing, critical thinking, cultural and religious history, and languages are part of Ashesi's core vocational curriculum," Davidson told us. Students who major in computer science, business, management information systems, or engineering "take yearlong seminars on leadership, ethics, and collaboration."[12] In 2018, the President of Ghana granted Ashesi a Charter to operate as a fully autonomous institution, the youngest university to have achieved such recognition, and one of five private universities in Ghana to have a Charter.[13]

Another approach, as suggested by Joseph Aoun, President of Northeastern University, Boston, is for the universities to consider themselves as lifelong learning institutions and cater to students who are threatened by technological change. Universities are recognized as "not merely in the specific businesses of undergraduate education, graduate education, and research—although all of these remain vitally important. Rather, they are in the larger business of lifelong learning."[14] In the lifelong learning business model, universities codevelop programs in partnership with employers and industry representatives. This means that they need to invite the representatives, understand their needs, and incorporate their requirements into the curriculum.

Northeastern University worked with employers to develop a master's degree to allow its liberal arts graduates to work as computer scientists. The 12-month program is embedded with placement opportunity with technology-focused companies. As Aoun explained, "Learners gain new high-tech skills—for example, in big-data analytics—by tackling content that is chunked out into on-the-job projects. These projects are coupled with online learning units to help learners master the latest technologies. Further, the programme leverages learners' experiences in the liberal arts, integrating these with their newfound talents, giving them an edge

---

[12] Ibid., p. 244.
[13] Extracted from https://ashesi.edu.gh/about.html on May 13, 2020.
[14] Aoun, "*Robot-Proof*," pp. 118–119.

on communication and critical thinking—crucial skills for management positions."[15]

Northeastern University shows that it is not impossible to blend business and humanities. Students can take courses to understand the operations of Wall Street, blend a little of tech and a lot of the empathetic, inquisitive skills that were picked up in liberal education. The key to success is to have the courage to explore, the willingness to learn after university, and the ability to put all the pieces together. Taking the advice from C.P. Snow, Northeastern University respects the "two cultures," the sciences and the humanities.[16]

- Impart Digital Skills and Technology Know-How Students Need

A great deal of work in the future will involve information management and information technology. Occupational groups most affected by computers or use computers more are most likely to experience the greatest increase in relative wage paid to educated and skilled workers.

Hence, students would benefit from learning about robotics and artificial intelligence—discuss how to use them at work and the opportunities surrounding their use to keep organizations relevant and competitive—and computing and digital-related skills—to secure jobs especially when companies have to deal with employment adjustment through attrition and labor turnover as a result of workers' retirement.

---

[15] Ibid., pp. 123–124.

[16] C.P. Snow, an English novelist and physical chemist, delivered "The Two Cultures" lecture in 1959. In the lecture, Snow described the relationship between the sciences and the humanities, and asked that schools and universities incorporate both branches of knowledge into the curriculum. He lamented that students were specialized in their area of students and had become "vastly ignorant" to the extent that "we have lost even the pretence of a common culture." He wrote "Persons educated with the greatest intensity we know can no longer communicate with each other on the plane of their major intellectual concern. This is serious for our creative, intellectual, and above all, our normal life." Snow, "*The Two Cultures*," 60.

Students would also benefit from learning about data analytics. With digital devices, social media and the Internet, there will be loads of data and information for the companies to collect and digest. To make sense of the data and information, companies will need data analyst to explore the shopping habits of consumers, identity potential clients, anticipate sales and future trends, and deliver the information and analysis in an easy-to-understand manner. The output of statistical models and algorithms will grow as a source of input and information to assist decision making. Students of all disciplines will have to be well versed in data analysis to contribute to the working environment.

In the world of computers and smartphones, coding or computer programming is the other type of literacy that students and the future workforce should acquire. Coding is an integral part of the Internet of Things ecosystem.[17] Like Mathematics, coding teaches us how to think, break down problems, and design ways to solve simple and complex issues. Mathematics is not just for Mathematicians. Likewise, coding is not just for coders. Coding can be regarded as a foundational skill, like writing and reading, to learn more about the world around us; one that is surrounded by computers and smartphones. The computer program has parallels to writing, argued Annette Vee. Vee wrote, "It is socially situation, the symbolic system that enables new kind of expressions as well as scaling up of pre-existing forms of communication. Like writing, the programme has been a fundamental tool and method to organise information."[18]

Computer code has structured in much of today's communication, including word processing, the World Wide Web, social networking, digital videos, and mobile phone production and application. During an interview, Steve Jobs equated computer programming as a liberal art, a subject that everyone should learn in schools. Organizations like code.org are doing just that. They are dedicated to expanding access to computer

---

[17] Internet of Thing means that any object in the world—cars, human body parts, electrical appliances, and others—can be assigned a network IP to connect to the network. When things can be digitally identified, we need to know how to communicate with them.

[18] Vee, "*Coding Literacy*," p. 3.

science in schools, developing a computer science curriculum at all levels. By seeing the program through writing and literature, schools should make coding a subject to teach, in various courses, including media, arts and humanities, library studies, biotech, finance, information science, political science, business, and literature.

In sum, having the opportunities to explore new technologies in the higher education institutions can help students to experience more meaningful learning, to figure out what they might be interested in, and to build the core skills and knowledge that students need when they join the workforce. With increase in the use of technology and digital platforms in business operations, learning how technology works and having the right digital skills will prepare students for a variety of work environments.

- Teach Students How to Learn

In addition to teaching relevant subjects and offering relevant courses, education institutions should equip students with the ability to learn. This is especially important when the nature of the skills is still uncertain and nonstandardized (think about getting ready for Industrial Revolution 4.0). James Beeson makes this point in his book *Learning by Doing*.[19] The general skills and knowledge are helpful to the students to learn in a new environment. For example, educated graphic designers could have acquired general skills and competency developed in schools to learn new technologies of websites and mobile apps. They might not have learned these specific technologies in schools, but the education received would give them the ability to teach themselves new skills on the job.

- Allow Students to Obtain a Degree at Their Own Pace

As jobs become more automated and integrated with rapidly changing technology, individuals will need to learn and relearn in different ways and various career stages to remain relevant and competitive. Universities

---

[19] Beeson, "*Leaning by Doing.*"

have to allow people, who want to access learning opportunities, to obtain a degree at their own pace.

Because the students are keen to participate in the labor market and some of them with family responsibility, they will not wish to undertake the full degree full time. They prefer to stack-up modules, one at a time with breaks in between. Working and schooling simultaneously is the preferred option, switching from work and study depending on opportunity. University has to work with businesses, extend learning support and candidature period to students as learning will not be confined to the education provider. Universities can consider provision of nano-degrees, competency-based education, or microcredentials—a certification in the form of badges to indicate competency in a specific skill.

- Develop Soft Skills Students and Employers Need

Success is no longer about reproducing content knowledge, but about extrapolating from what we know and applying that knowledge to novel situations. To meet this challenge, education providers must enable students to acquire critical thinking, problem solving, communication, and collaboration skills they will need to be successful at work and in life.

University education plays an important role by giving students an opportunity to live away from their parents, and develop connections to faculty, other students, and people in the community—which is very often—far from where they grew up. It is often difficult to cope with the diversity of campus culture and home culture. But once the challenge has been overcome, university education offers a great opportunity for cultural and social learning experience which is particularly useful for students who work in cross-cultural teams.

The National Association of Colleges and Employers' annual survey of skills that employers want in college graduate hires has pointed toward attributes such as teamwork, communication, and problem-solving competencies. Sharon Paronto and Mayuresh Kelkar noted that employers tend to be more satisfied with employees who are creative and display critical thinking and leadership skills than those who have strong technical skills and knowledge.[20] Google, for example, wants employees to be collaborative and socially accountable to each other. Fast-growing new companies, wrote George Anders, "needed generalists who knew a little bit of tech—and a lot about human nature."[21]

The World Economic Forum has identified creativity, persuasion, collaboration, adaptability, and emotional intelligence as the five most in-demand soft skills.[22]

The National Institute of Technological Education of Argentina surveyed 876 private companies in 2016 to find the skills they would want from high school graduates. The response was clear; they wanted people with soft skills such as teamwork, willingness to learn new things, adaptability to change, and a strong work ethic.[23]

Understanding and appreciating the value of soft skills is helpful so that education providers can design curriculum and assessment tasks that are aimed at building student strengths in these areas. Do this well and students will be better prepared to meet the requirements of hiring companies. For example, universities can allow time for creative projects. This means empowering students to make decisions like what to explore, allocate tasks, manage their own time, and allow for failures. The role of teachers is to coach students, create conditions for innovation, and encourage students to engage in deeper levels of thinking. Teachers should not offer ready-made solutions.[24]

---

[20] Paranto and Kelkar, "*Employer Satisfaction With Job Skills of Business College Graduates and its Impact on Hiring Behavior.*"

[21] Anders, "*You Can Do Anything*," p. 8.

[22] Blue, "*5 Things We Know About the Jobs of the Future.*"

[23] Cited from Oppenheimer, "*The Robots Are Coming!*" p. 251.

[24] In classroom teaching, teachers typically out-talked the entire class of students; the bulk of the teacher-talking was to tell and instruct. The prevalent view amongst teachers is that student ideas are disruptive, and hence they are quickly dismissed. Consequently, student comes to develop a pattern of learning; wait for the teacher to ask questions, raise your hand, wait for the teacher to call you, share your response and wait for the teacher to tell you if you response is correct, appropriate or otherwise. But this is not how the world operates or how the future of work looks like. At work, individuals are expected to work together in a complex social system. They have to response quickly, solving complex and

In regard to assessments, they do not have to be in the form of examinations. Higher education institutions could introduce alternative assessments such as portfolio development, reflective report, and project work to accommodate different learning styles, to allow for multidisciplinary solutions, and to move away from focusing on the recalling ability of students to the ability of a students in analyzing and synthesizing a set of information for a desired outcome. Learning and assessment could be application-based and global-orientated; getting students to design a software for a firm where students could consider multiple perspectives when solving a problem. Universities could collaborate with businesses, nonprofit organizations, and public sector corporations to give students the opportunity to work on industry projects and apply the knowledge and skills that they learn.

Problem solving in the real-world or in a simulated environment encourages students to look at the problems from different perspectives, resembling the actual working environments that are holistic, nonlinear, and multidimensional. The future of work will require employees to demonstrate skills that even intelligent machines or digital devices cannot perfect as well as humans.

---

interdisciplinary, open-ended problems, making innovative use of information, knowledge and opportunities a well creative and problem-solving thinking skills important. Organizations around the world understand that the bottom-line success relies on the ability to innovate to deliver the best product, process and service, and that before any innovation can take place, the ideas must be generated by individuals and teams, not machines. To prepare students for the future of work, educators have to see 'ideas' differently. To improve student problem-solving ability and promote the development of curiosity and ingenuity, students must be encouraged to come up with ideas. Any ideas that involve construction of new meaning is creative. Creativity is not an end, but a means toward ends such as improving problem-solving ability and thinking skills. A bad idea from students can be creative, and should not be dismissed outright. A great educator helps the students to see why the idea is not a good one, offering suggestions to increase its potentiality.

- Go Blended and Adapt to Pedagogy of Online Teaching

While information technology is increasingly influential, some schools are still a long way from exploiting what technology can do in formal teaching to complement established practices. Higher learning institutions need to rethink about the source of learning.

The use of information technology can increase student motivation—for example, by gaining the attention of media-savvy students through the use of multimedia. It can also address more learning styles. The use of animations, graphics, and digital images helps to stimulate visual learning whereas the use of sound, music, playback, and recordings helps students who prefer to learn via spoken word, sound, or music. Students who prefer more active forms of learning—kinesthetic learners—can learn by operating a variety of devices such as a pen to control software or the mouse or keyboard to draw and write. Students in a large measure have integrated technology and the Internet into most aspects of their lives. They would expect the same from the higher education institutions when it comes to educational provision and experiences.

The use of online games or computer-based entertainment software to promote learning in schools is worth considering. While playing games has been linked to aggressive thoughts and feelings and less pro-social behavior, one should also recognize the educational values of games.[25] In his book *What Video Games Have to Teach Us About Learning and Literary*, James Paul Gee listed a total of 36 learning principles and concluded that games could motivate students to learn and keep on learning.[26] One of the reasons for this is that in a game, the problems are usually presented in an organized and well-structured manner so that students who generate hypotheses can test out at the next level or when they start the game all over. Moreover, games could simulate real-world scenarios and allow students to work in groups to communicate, collaborate, and evaluate

---

[25] Anderson and Bushman, "*Effects of Violent Video Games on Aggressive Behavior, Aggressive Cognition, Aggressive Affect, Psychological Arousal, and Prosocial Behavior*"; Anderson, Gentile, and Buckley, "*Violent Video Game Effects on Children and Adolescents.*"

[26] Gee, "*What Video Games Have to Teach Us About Learning and Literacy.*"

multiple perspectives and solutions. Given the popularity of online games, learning institutions could explore the use of games in the course to get students to practice the skills of analysis, synthesis, evaluation, and problem solving. Ultimately, it is about striking a balance between learning through gamification and excessive engagement in games and the role of educators is to help students minimize the negative effects while maximizing learning experiences.

The education institutions should consider adopting learning tools and techniques such as flipped classroom and blended learning. The Socratic method of guiding the students with the answers put the students into a passive mode of learning. In a blended class, students spend time on asynchronous materials (e.g., from YouTube, TedTalks, and Khan Academy) and other digital learning resources to help them with the coursework. Students still have to learn the same contents as they would in the traditional class. But class time is devoted to discussion and problem solving, in translation from lecture to discussion, and active learning, and to get students to be more involved in the research-oriented and thought-based learning process. The layout of the classroom can be changed from neat rows of chairs and tables to flexible learning arrangement to enable collaborative learning to take place.

Santiago Iniquez de Onzono, Dean of IE Business School and President of IE University identified a number of advantages of blended learning. First, blended learning is flexible where students can access the courses where and when they want. Second, it permits collaborative learning as technologies and the Internet allow for a wide access to peers and other learners. Third, technologies and the Internet allow for continuous feedback thereby keeping the momentum to learn. Fourth, online delivery helps the education providers create new markets and export their programs to other parts of the world.

De Onzono is an authoritative figure to comment on online learning. The IE University's Global Online MBA is a top-ranked qualification in the QS and Financial Times rankings.[27] In his book *The Learning Curve*,

---

[27] De Onzono, "*The Learning Curve*," p. 77. Students can complete the program in 17 or 24 months, pursuing it either online or through blended methodology with face-to-face sessions in Madrid.

De Onzono shares the factors contributing to the program's success. One of the factors is strong involvement of teaching staff in the process of combining teaching with technology. He understood that the teaching faculty would lack the qualification and experience to deliver their lessons online. This was dealt with by providing intensive training and support to the educators. In addition, the educators who produced the teaching materials in the traditional setting were used to develop online teaching materials, working closely with the Program Directors and technicians. By teaching the materials they developed, there is greater accountability and familiarity, contributing to improved teaching quality. The university did not subcontract the task. Because of the additional work involved, including time spent answering students' queries, the educators were paid more.

Blended learning is no longer a new initiative. Most schools are already merging face-to-face teaching with online lessons. To set a school apart from the rest, De Onzono advised schools to conduct "on-going training" for teachers "to improve their ability to combine technology with educational delivery" and develop "new contents, formats, and network by making use of the growing number of new resources and relationships available through the Internet."[28] Critically, education providers should adopt blended delivery only if it serves a cause that is worthwhile in itself, and not as a way to drive cost down at the expense of quality creation. Education providers should not lose sight of its true function—to ensure that students learn and that they have met the stipulated learning outcomes of the subjects and courses. It is not, and never has been, to simply generate revenue or make a profit.

In sum, we can either do something about the disconnection between university curriculum and the future of work or surrender student schooling experience. The stakes are just that. That said, it is worth nothing that externally imposed educational mandates often fail to take into consideration the realities of classroom teaching. Educators feel overwhelmed with contradictory demands, exacerbating the barrier to school initiative. Mandating that teachers add multidisciplinary perspectives into the

---

[28] Ibid., p. 78.

curriculum, to take an example, may only increase the feelings of discontentment. A better approach is to develop a multidisciplinary unit or committee to advice educators who are themselves directly involved in the design of the curriculum so that they are aware of and begin addressing common barriers to create meaningful and effective change in their classrooms. By the time they engage their students in the classroom, they would have developed robust beliefs, images, and assumptions to address any problematic behaviors and assumptions about multidisciplinary education in the classroom. In short, educators need to understand multidisciplinary approach in order to embrace it. This begins with a clear understanding of what multidisciplinary study is, why it is important and how we can develop the curriculum.

CHAPTER 5

Passion for Learning

Higher education is often associated to good job prospects, and of course, better salaries. It is an entrenched perception—propelling young people to pursue relentlessly academic qualifications. University degrees or equivalent vocational certificates are viewed to play a part in remuneration. But as Jeffrey Sachs pointed out, there is a difference between earning more income and "relentlessly craving for more income." Sachs wrote "Individuals with a high materialistic orientation, for whom earning and spending money are a central aim of life, are systematically far less happy and secure than nonmaterialism."[1] To Sachs, students find happiness if they can strike a right balance between learning what interests them and the necessity to acquire a certain educational qualification to earn (but not crave for) more income.

We make decisions to maximize our utility. There are individuals who learn for learning's sake. They are willing to spend several years of their life pursuing a higher education qualification, committing resources and juggling work, family, and study. The will to learn injects in them educational energy and propel the sustainable steadiness to complete a program. In comparison to those choosing to enroll into a program to get a job or please parents, the former stands a better chance of accomplishing academic success.

---

[1] Sachs, "*The Price of Civilisation*," p. 166. Sachs highlighted the enticements of modern media—commercial advertising, public relations campaigns—which have "remoulded" our psyches to want more and more consumption. The key to achieve long-term happiness is to adopt the middle path. Sachs told us, "The essential teaching of both Buddha and Aristotle is that the path of moderation is the key to fulfilment but is hard won and must be pursued through lifelong diligence, training, and reflection" (ibid., p. 62).

Passion for learning infuses in one the positivity needed to attain success in life. When pursing our passion, we embark on a journey, rather than a destination, to reach our maximum potential and fulfill the purpose of life. It is about identifying the vision deep inside us, about things that we are born to do and appeal to our highest ideals.

It is worth noting that in the beginning of the Christian era, passion was condemned as a sin. Passion for power, material gains, and lust were believed to have led the ruling elite in Western Europe to wreak havoc on the people they ruled over. Albert Hisrchman articulated this point this way: "To imagine an authority *ex machina* that would somehow suppress the misery and havoc men inflict on each other as a result of their passions means in effect to wish away, rather than to solve, the very difficulties that have been discovered. It is perhaps for this reason that the repressive solution did not survive the detailed analysis of the passions in the seventeenth century."[2]

Passion was viewed more positively at the time where capitalism offered a viable economic system for growth and development. In particular, Adam Smith's "invisible hand" implies that when men pursue their passion either knowingly or unknowingly, they will often be led, as if by an invisible hand, to contribute to the public good. Adam Smith famously reminded us, two-and-a-half centuries ago, that we do not get our daily bread through the kindness of the baker, but rather because the baker needs to make money. Containing the destructive nature of passion apparently requires passions to be set against one another. This is reflective of a large part of the world we are living in.

Who Are the Passionate Learners?

"All men desire knowledge," wrote Aristotle in Metaphysics.[3] Men, unlike animals, are able to learn and store information in our brain. The faculty of memory contributes to human intelligence. It is from memory that we acquire experience and the ability to make better decisions and judgment.

---

[2] Hirchman, "*The Passions and the Interests*," p. 16.
[3] Cited from Allen, "*Greek Philosophy*," p. 307.

Learning is therefore the means to an end, and not the end itself.[4] As we participate more vigorously in a two-way dialogue between us and the outside world, the ability to contextualize and seeing and appreciating one thing in terms of another is especially important to lead a fruitful and satisfying life. Surely this is what intelligence is all about—the term is literally the Latin provenance of "understanding." Why not celebrate the uniqueness of homo sapiens and take full advantage of it?

A person who loves learning is committed to delve deeply into the pool of knowledge. The learner considers the brain as the tool-chest or a working tool (not merely a storage of knowledge and information) to use and apply the knowledge when it is necessary to do so. Aristotle associates the pursuit of happiness to acquiring the ability to converse, read, develop intellect, and seek virtue. Love of learning prescribes the ways in which we engage knowledge and information.

Enthusiasm—open displays of excitement of learning—are manifestations of a passionate learner. The learner is drawn to learning, seeing it as a kind of self-indulgence rather than as a duty. A passionate learner asks tons of questions, and (like Socrates) is more willing to admit that he or she does not know everything than anyone else. Passionate learners desire to acquire skills of composition and argument. They listen and participate actively in classroom. They arrive punctually for classes, read the assigned readings, and complete the assignments and homework.

They want to write persuasively and be able to solve unknown problem confidently. They respect learning for its own sake, to seek truth and make sense of the information. They become their own teacher, learning to take care of their own affairs—economic, social, and psychological.

---

[4] Homo sapiens are the knowing man, the brainy species that acquires knowledge and uses information. Several breakthroughs such as the creation of writing, reading and now the electronic media or what Steven Pinker calls the "supernova of knowledge" will continue to redefine "what it means to be human." Pinker wrote; "To be aware of one's country and its history of the diversity of customs and beliefs across the globe and through the ages, of the blunders and triumphs of past civilisations, of the microcosms of cells and atoms and the macrocosms of planets and galaxies, of the ethereal reality of number and logic and pattern—such awareness truly lifts us to a higher plan of consciousness. It is a gift of belonging to a brainy species with a long history." See Pinker, "*Enlightened Now*," p. 233.

They inspire to exceed the minimum requirements as stipulated in the course, incorporating aspects of enjoyment and liberty into learning to the extent that distinguishing between work, learning, and play is often impossible. They are open to new points of view and willing to suspend judgment until they have understood and thought about what they listened and read. Above all, passionate learners are excited to see a mind at work—a clear great mind, thinking, organizing ideas, making an argument, selecting the evidence, the sentences, and the emphasis to communicate the meaning to another mind.

While the inner urge to learn and acquire knowledge is strong, there can be no doubt that the inner development is also influenced by the external environment such as the desire to win and defeat others in the competitive world. Students are generally sensitive to how they are compared with their peers. If this is to serve as the only reason for learning, the interest is misdirected; guided by the desire for winning rather than for inner satisfaction. For the inner urge to develop unmolested or free of any hindrances, it is desirable that the students focus not on defeating the object in view, for example, in the race to be among the top in the class, but to view learning as a means to lead to the end that is genuine and enduring.

A passionate learner does not totally ignore reward or extrinsic values that education can bring. Educational credentials help to secure a good job and salary, but a passionate learner pays greater attention to the usage value of education, in addition to the exchange value, associated with schooling. For example, the education received in schools can be lifelong; skills of learning to learn, for example, is helpful for more effective adaptation to a constantly changing environment. Some would seek short-term courses to learn a specific skill. Some would enroll into a program to explore various related subjects or disciplines. Some would want to join the classes to read classic to appreciate human wisdom. Some may desire breadth; others may prefer depth. Acquisition of useful knowledge is a strong motivating factor itself. The decision to enroll in a program in an education institution reflects the person's pure love for schooling, and association with the education system as one that is responsible, promising, and joyous.

Education has an intrinsic worth as Frank Furedi has argued. By that, he refers to the "valuation of cultural accomplishments through which society renews itself and acquires the intellectual and moral resources necessary to understand itself and face the future."[5] Learning responses to the inner self because the learner is inexorably drawn to or is fascinated with the learning. In an extreme instance, learning is not seen as a duty, or obligation, or responsibility, but a decision to engage in more than anything else in the world.

Why Is Passion for Learning Important?

Passion for learning is about the desire for knowledge and skills so that participants can make more informed decisions. It is about helping students to understand the world better. The good news is that passion for learning appears high on the list of reasons for enrolling for colleges. In the United States, the Higher Education Research Institute at the University of California, Los Angeles, administers the National Survey of Freshmen each year, to hundreds of thousands of incoming college students. Respondents were asked "What do you hope to get out of college?" Getting a job ranks high in the list of what they want out of college. In 2014, 86.1 percent of them said this was what they want. In that year, students also wanted "to gain a general education and appreciation of ideas" (70.6%), "to make me a more cultured person" (46.6%), and "to learn more things that interest me" (82.2%), suggesting that students wanted to learn.[6] While we can expect that a pragmatic student with a strong passion to learn is also attracted to reward and success, money and praises are not finality, the end and the ultimate goal of education.

When one is intensely engaged in learning, it boosts the level of satisfaction, and happiness will blossom. As Richard Layard said in his coauthored book *The Origins of Happiness*, self-reported life satisfaction can be a good measure of happiness.[7] Learning subjects like Geography and Philosophy is one thing. Learning to love Geography and Philosophy is another. A passionate learner will be inclined to review and revise the contents of a subject, and with each repetition, it elevates the satisfaction

---

[5] Furedi, "*Wasted*," p. 20.
[6] Quoted from Blum, "*I Love Learning; I Hate School*," p. 66.
[7] Clark, Fleche, Layard, Powdthavee, and Ward, "*The Origins of Happiness*."

level. In addition, reusing the information motivates the learner to repeat his behavior—learning. This cycle makes studying and learning innate abilities. Others may try to discourage the learner or laugh at the person or the learner may find difficulties coping with the studies, but as long as the learner feels the inner urge, he will persist despite the outside interferences.

On the contrary, a student who lacks the inner urge will try to convince the teacher by bluffing or even by cheating. The student lacks the motivation because he does not see the value of learning the subject or that learning requires too much time and effort. Teachers may have to resort to coercion. Very often, authoritarian teaching attitude rests on the assumption that students are naturally less motivated to complete their schoolwork, and thus, require sternness and punishment to push them to do a given task. What is the impact of coercion on learning? A coerced student who is not ready to absorb the subject contents will not find learning satisfying. The student is also not likely to learn rapidly and can easily get distracted. Because the student is coerced into doing the job, the student is unlikely to receive praise from people surrounding the learner. The student does not receive the encouragement needed and will gradually lose more interest in learning. Coercion in this regard will not help. However, if the student has potential but does not know it yet, a certain amount of coercion can be useful to overcome the initial challenges and rejections. With the right environment and support, the student may discover the interest and passion for the subject, bringing enough satisfaction for the learner to pursue the subject more. In such circumstances, coercion may help.

As William Heard Kilpatrick told us, when a student finds satisfaction in learning, learning takes place.[8] Clearly, piquing interest and helping students discover their passion is possibly one of the most important functions of an education. Against the suggestion that the inner urge is fixated and that it is impenetrable by an outside force is the possibility for schools in general and teachers in particular to subject their students to new realities and challenges. Students are different in interests, assumptions, and interpretations of news and events. What is needed are convincing stories

---

[8] Kilpatrick, "*Foundations of Method.*"

impressed upon the students about the beauty of learning and to help students believe in their intelligences, interests, and abilities. Students can learn by accommodating and reflecting on the information and experiences to pick up new ideas and interests. The nature of questioning matters. Often, teachers concentrate on what students ought to do to realize their dreams. Some students may be more persuaded if they are asked to consider what could do to them if they failed to learn, for example, what would happen if you do not learn?

With passion and interest, the learning progress can be extremely enjoyable to the self. This is what life ought to be. In the process of living itself, the person learns to take charge of what in the person's own mind, to discover what really matters to him or her and avoid being overly burdened by socially conditioned goals. Mihaly Cszszentmihalyi developed the concept of flow to illustrate the optimal experience, referring flow as the "state in which people are so involved in the activity that nothing else matters; the experience itself is so enjoyable that people will do it even at great loss, for the sheer sake of doing it."[9] Cszszentmihalyi rightly pointed out that life is a changing process, in which nothing is fixed. Students find richness in life by letting the flow to take over and be fascinated with experience that life can bring. The experience will direct them toward goals and desires that they are only dimly aware of.

In a competitive environment, students are externally driven right from the early days of schooling; namely to do well in school and major in a certain discipline not because they want to pursue them or because they expect to reap economic reward from it in the future but to satisfy the needs of their parent and the society. Sadly, without the flow, the excitement of schooling will gradually decline, and eventually, schooling may be perceived as a waste of time.

For flow to take place, do we need schools? After all, learning can occur everywhere and can take various forms. One can learn in book clubs, listening to talks online, talking to others, playing games, building

---

[9] Cszszentmihalyi, "*Flow*," p. 4. Educators have been researching on integrating curiosity and interest as positive motivations for learning, positioning them as a model for cognitive and academic development. See Peterson and Hidi, "*Curiosity and Interest*"; Alexander, "*Seeking Common Ground.*"

things, and the list goes on. If people wish to learn, they would gather together. If all is needed is more information, everyone with an Internet connection will be blissfully happy. What can schooling bring? Why do we need to go to schools? These are possibly questions that one would ask at one point or another.

Implications for Higher Education

Learning institutions like the universities offer the opportunity to learn and share ideas with peers and experts, reaching out to those who have deep knowledge about the subject and also who could teach effectively. This is particularly important in the age of information abundance. With the introduction of books in the early days and the Internet more recently, humans are constantly exposed with information, some of which are technically difficult and challenging to decipher and understand. In the age of the Internet, information floods the corridor of learning. The influx of information is channeled and filtered into the different tiers of the educational system, with learning institutions being the platform for learners to immense and engage in an ecosystem of learning, sharing, and teaching.

Various filters have been introduced to help us locate the required information. In the digital age, we have search engines like Google and other navigational tools to help us identify and look for the desired information as quickly as possible. Schools serve as a filer as well. Schools group information into disciplines and by levels in terms of their level of complexity, and teachers step in to help students understand, decipher, and apply the knowledge in their everyday life and at work.

But there is a difference between schooling and search engines in relation to their roles as filters. Nicholas Carr identified two forms of information overload—situational overload and ambient overload. Situational overload "is the needle-in the-haystack problem" where students need to locate a particular piece of information in order to answer a question, and that piece of information is "buried in the bunch of other pieces of information."[10] The traditional filters as well as modern filters like search

---

[10] Carr, *"Utopia Is Creepy and Other Provocations,"* pp. 90–91.

engines are rather effective in solving this kind of problem. In schools, teachers help students to identify the right information, focus on certain contents in class to enable the students to learn, and apply certain knowledge rightfully and meaningfully.

Ambient overload, on the other hand, does not involve needles in haystacks. Rather "it involves haystack-sized piles of needles." It refers to the phenomenon where students are "surrounded by so much information that is of immediate interest to us that we feel overwhelmed by the never-ending pressure of trying to keep up with it all." This occurs in the digital age when we click on links after links and keep on opening new tabs, checking e-mails and social media feeds, and scanning for Amazon and Netflix recommendations—"the pile of interesting information never shrinks." Here, the modern filters such as search engines do not only organize the information for us. Instead, they push more and more information to us as alerts, updates, and so on. That said, the way forward is not to block student access to the Internet nor deprive students from gaining knowledge or acquiring information for varied purposes. We need more schooling. The organizational pattern of learning institutions can help by mediating the connection between ambient overload and time pressure resulted from it and the need to make sense of the information through deep and critical thinking.

We all can agree that students are not alike. Students have a different motive for enrolling into a course. Some are compliance with school rules and regulations, others are more argumentative. Some are courageous to learn outside of the syllabus, others are exam-focused. Some are extroverts, others are happier to study by themselves. Learning injects pleasure and pain into the learner. Schools and teachers can play a significant role in inculcating the habit of right actions; the virtue of acquiring, practicing, and applying what has been learned in a constructive way. Humans are not born to be good or bad, but they need to be guided by authoritative figures. Frank Furedi wrote that "students become motivated to learn through a combination of different factors ... Within the school it is the authoritative guidance and, in some cases, the inspiration provided by teachers that has helped to motivate young people. The aspiration to learn and the motivation to study are outcomes of family and community influence and the authoritative leadership provided by schools and teachers."[11]

In this regard, one of the goals of education is to help the person to become a human being, as fully human as possible. Abraham Maslow called this the process of self-actualization. Self-actualization is about "going through an arduous and demanding period of preparation in order to realise one's possibilities."[12] The goal of education, Maslow wrote, is the "human goal, the humanistic goal, the goal as far as human beings are concerned—is ultimately the self-actualisation of a person, the becoming fully human, the development of the fullest height that the human species can stand up to or that the particular individual can come to. In a less technical way, it is helping the person to become the best that he is able to become."[13] Intrinsic learning is learning to be a human being in general. The role of schools and teachers is to help students discover what it is that they want to do with their life, which is almost synonymous with finding their career.

John Gardner, former President of the Carnegie Corporation and of the Carnegie Foundation for the Advancement of Teaching, saw the educational purpose as one that concerns with the worth of the individual and importance of individual fulfillment.[14] This means that the pursuit of education must be seen as concerning self-discovery to realize the best of oneself and to be the best person that he could be. The purpose of education is less about material gains and even intellectual development but to spur emotional, character, moral, and spiritual growth. Therefore, schools and teachers play a crucial role in instilling the attitude, spirit, and mindset toward continuous reexamination and reshaping of oneself through an indefinite learning process.

It can then be argued that schools represent an ideal place for reflection; to wonder, probe, and analyze the meaning of experience and of

---

[11] Furedi, "*Wasted*," p. 11.
[12] Maslow, "*The Farther Reaches of Human Nature*," p. 46.
[13] Ibid., pp. 162–163.
[14] Gardner, "*Excellence*."

life.¹⁵ To reflect, students need the time and space to think about what they have been through in class to discover their passions and interests through listening, reading, writing, and interacting with like-minded persons. Reflection is largely a personal endeavor but an important activity to undertake to step back and ponder on the interesting ideas, beliefs, and difficult questions that could ultimately expose students to alternative decisions and ways of behaving that can profoundly change their course of life toward the better.

The problem in the current economic system is that learning, and education are often seen as the means to getting a job. Schools and colleges are built on the assumption that students should work hard, get good grades, and get good jobs in the private or public sector. The demand for education is driven by economic interest. Universities pride themselves by achieving high graduate employment rate and good starting salary for their graduates. When the graduates are not employed, schools are blamed for ill-preparing the students and undeservedly labelled as lesser-known institutions with a distance-footing with brand-name ones. Hence, higher education institutions are in a hurry to secure employment for their graduates even before they students graduate from the courses, ignoring the existence of alternative reasons for learning. Students are often never told that learning itself is rightful and richly deserving.¹⁶

---

[15] Some may argue that university is the place to learn and not to make money. Stefan Collini, for example, advised, "If you want to make money, go into business. If you want to learn how to make money, go to business school. If you want to learn what money is and how it has functioned and what might be the point of making a lot of money, go to university." See Collini, "*Speaking of Universities*," p. 79. Mixing the two objectives—making money and learning what money is—gives rise to the paradox of real learning. To gain employment in the job market, students opt for easy pass subjects and pick lecturers who are lenient in marking and left the university with the feeling that they have not been educated.

[16] Neil Postman has argued that the current crisis in education system is derived from the lack of a unifying narratives like those in the past as found in texts such as the Old Testament, the New Testament, and Koran and the Bhagavad Gita. The narratives, incorporating the lives of ancestors and set in a historical context, provide at least three benefits: (i) "help students to see that knowledge is a stage in human development, with a past and a future," (ii) "acquaint students with the

Instead, they are motivated to achieve success by working harder and longer. Students put in the effort to study because they want to get a degree and receive praise and approval from parents and hiring companies. They learn for examinations and not from a love of learning. They strive to obtain higher grades or even attempt to cheat in the examinations to give them the extra edge in the pursuit of success. But reward does not always lead to desirable behavior as Edward Deci's research told us. In one of his experiments, Deci placed college students into two groups. One group was offered a monetary reward for solving a puzzle. The other group was asked to solve the puzzle minus the monetary reward. Deci found that the former showed less interest in the puzzle than the other group, a result that has been replicated elsewhere. Rewarding had backfired. It directed the attention of students to pursue a single passion and exclude everything else.[17]

Anxiety and concerns about succeeding at schools prevent students from experiencing joy when learning. They focus on getting good grades, spending much of the time in schools to master the test format, regurgitating "answers" with the goal of reproducing the information in examinations. Getting good grades is a pragmatic motive. Grades are used for entry into the next level of schooling. But a student with good grades does not necessarily mean that actual learning has taken place, or if the student has enjoyed learning. High achieving students can learn to play the game of schools like cleverly guessing the questions that will be asked in the examinations, pleasing teachers, and threatening their teachers with poor evaluation score to secure high grades without learning anything. The lucky one cheats in the examination or plagiarize in the coursework and escapes undetected.

I like Susan Blum's depiction of schools as a garden where students are carefully nurtured to bring the best out of students. School as a garden

---

people the ideas that comprise cultural literacy—that is to say, give them some understanding of where their ideas come from and how we came by them," and (iii) "that error is no disgrace, that it is the agency through which we increase understanding." See Postman, "*The End of Education*," p. 125.

[17] Deci, "*Effects of Externally Mediated Rewards on Intrinsic Motivation.*" See also Gneezy and List, "*The Why Axis.*"

is different from factory schools (some students may equate to schools as war or a prison) where students are deemed as uniformed materials that are put through a fixated set of procedures. The factory model as Blum told us can result in "unhappiness, mental illnesses, unhealthy competition, dropping out, and superficial performance."[18] Conversely, in a garden, gardeners decide what crops to plant, spending lengthy time to prepare. Gardening requires constant supply and control of water. Gardeners submit themselves to varied goals of production and modify them according to weather conditions and demand. They are involved in supervising the production, working themselves into exhaustion but with much enjoyment, knowing that the plants are nurtured with care and through careful thought right from the start. The school as a garden metaphor is about working "with the tendencies of human beings (tendencies toward movement and sociality); we have to produce diverse results in order to ensure that, whatever comes, some will be prepared to grow; we have to plan as best we can for a variety of users; we have to consider the social and economic contexts."[19] By tapping into students' energy and allowing them to follow the natural tendencies and tearing down the school walls, students' passions and interests are cultivated to reap satisfaction and promote learning.

Up to now, it has been assumed that students know what they are passionate about and have the freedom to pursue them. Knowing your passions and interests is a complicated matter. It is akin to knowing one's own self. In his book *The Ego Trick*, British philosopher Julian Baggini looks at how a sense of self emerges among us.[20] Baggini argued that the sense of self is developed through a collection of thoughts influenced by internal and external environments. It is not true that one has a core essence of self that stay with him. Rather, we accumulate experiences over time, interrelating and connecting the experiences with memory, belief, and sensation to form "you."

Does the self have the free will to determine what interests the person? The traditional idea is that we are the author of our own thoughts

---

[18] Blum, "*I Love learning, I Hate School*," p. 277.
[19] Ibid., p. 280.
[20] Baggini, "*The Ego Trick*."

and that we are conscious of our thoughts and actions. In a world where educational qualification does not serve as a signal to get a job, there is no worry but to enjoy life by pursuing your passion. Students learn what they want. But in reality, hiring companies rely on what students have learned in schools and the grades attained. We are influenced and rely on others, parents, teachers, and the society in general, to tell us what is good for us—sometimes also due to the lack of knowledge to enable us to make a proper choice. For example, to meet the needs of the society, governments have used monetary incentives to influence the choice of students in relation to the major to take at the university. In October 2010, for example, the UK government announced its plan to phase out teaching grants for courses in the arts, humanities, and social sciences, thereby making it more costly for students to pursue these courses, while suggested that in the future, sciences and mathematics courses would be funded wholly via tuition fees. In June 2020, the Australian federal government announced a "shake-up" of university fees to encourage students to take up courses in fields where employment is likely to grow, including agriculture, psychology, foreign languages, and Mathematics and away from those seen as having fewer employment prospects, like law, commerce, and humanities. What we want is often an ideal but in a realistic position, when students are confronted with the choice between passion and duty to meet parental and societal demands, duty prevails.

When it comes to education, politics matters. Political goals shape education policies and system that can potentially hinder the pursuit of passions and interests. In achieving the nationalist goals and the goal of economic development, students are taught and reminded time and time again to acquire certain knowledge that the state wants and thinks as important. The learning outcomes are predetermined by national and economic goals—prioritizing and incentivizing what to learn. Students are taught to cherish the cultural tradition or constantly reminded of the humiliation the nation suffered in the past. To catch-up with and overtake the rest, the state reorganizes and reforms the education system to train broad masses of people normally in the fields of sciences, technology, and engineering. Fields such as the arts and the humanities are considered as indulgences and luxuries that the nation cannot afford to focus on, depriving students to discover what they really want. The essence is that political objective takes precedence over all other aspects of education. Matters like selection of students and teachers, intake size of each cohort, and design of the courses and curriculum are treated according to the political consciousness. Academic indulgences have to wait, and subject to the economic and political reality of the nation. The mindset is based on premise that student represents an important asset to the nation. Therefore, for economic and political reasons, the education system has to be adjusted and developed in such a way that it facilitates the development of the nation and its society, and not the need of the individuals. At the same time, students are not at the age to determine the education they want. The consequence is that students are overwhelmed by confusions and conflicts, finding themselves unhappy with schooling.

The concept of free will is therefore a fallacy. Our actions are not a product of unimpeded choice. In his book *Free Will*, Sam Harris argued that our decisions are to a large extent made unconsciously. We made decisions in the brain some time before we consciously become aware of them. He wrote that "where our intentions themselves come from, and what determines their character in every instance, remains perfectly mysterious in subjective terms … We do not know what we intend to do until the intention itself arises. To understand this is to realise that we are not the author of our thoughts and actions in the way that people generally suppose."[21] It is an illusion therefore to think that we act freely, for example, in determining what interests us.

Hence, it is important to distinguish between choice and influence. Choice is a psychological, a perceptive power that we have. Influence is a hidden force that makes people want to obey, to impose, and to command possibly against their will. Influence can lead to a decision, but it

---

[21] Harris, "*Free Will*," p. 13. Harris illustrates his thesis with the example of choosing beer over wine. "Why did I order beer instead of wine? Because I prefer beer. Why do I prefer beer? I don't know, but I generally have no need to ask. Knowing that I like beer more than wine is all I need to know to function in a restaurant. Whatever the reason, I prefer one taste to the other. Is there freedom in this? None whatsoever. Would I magically reclaim my freedom if I decided to spite my preference and order wine instead? No, because the roots of this intention would be as obscure as the preference itself" (ibid., p. 60).

does not legitimize the choice. To have more freedom of choice, it entails a transformation of social relations of production. Until that happens, it is an illusion to expect students to have the freedom to pursue their passion and interest.

To conclude, the demand for education, whether it is derived from the Human Capital Theory[22] or Signaling Theory[23], places an emphasis

---

[22] In the "Human Capital Theory," the demand for education is associated with the belief that education attainment translates to higher wages and standard of living. The benchmark model was derived by Jacob Mincer, an economist from the University of Chicago, who regressed the natural logarithm of earnings against educational attainment and a host of other variables. The estimated coefficient for education such as years of schooling measures the percentage change in wage associated with an additional year of schooling. Mincer postulates that education is productivity enhancing, that is, each additional year of education brings about an improvement in productivity that provides the justification for employers to pay higher wages to the more education. Demand for education in this regard is a function of good future prospect. On average, Mincer found that the returns to education were about 10% worldwide with higher returns recorded for low-income and middle-income countries (returns to education in Asia was about the world average). Women received higher returns than men, and younger persons enjoyed higher returns than older workers. See Mincer, "*Schooling, Experience and Earnings.*" David Autor, an economist from the MIT, estimated that inflation-adjusted earnings of US men with a university degree rose about 50% from 1970 to 2010 whereas persons with some college but no degree experienced stagnant wages over these years. See Autor, "*Skills, Education, and the Rise of Earnings Inequality Among the 'Other 99 Percent.'*" In the case of Singapore, the rate of return to education showed high rate of return to tertiary education (polytechnic and university) as compared to the rate of return to secondary education. For each additional year of schooling, earnings for workers increased by an average of 13%. See Toh and Wong, "*Rates of Return to Education in Singapore*"; Sakellariou, "*Rates of Return to Investments in Formal and Technical/Vocational Education in Singapore*"; Yeo, Toh, Thangavelu, and Wong, "*Premium on Fields of Study.*"

[23] The "Signaling Theory" postulates that what most people most knew about is themselves. This is the case in many aspects of our life. Sellers know more about the quality of cars than the buyers; borrowers know more about their creditworthiness than the lenders. Specifically, Michael Spence was able to show how the able agents could improve the market outcome by taking costly action to signal information to poorly informed recipients. Spence's theory market signaling was first developed as his PhD thesis, and later published as a book. See Spence,

on the economic purpose, which includes getting a job and improving the standard of living, involving the making and spending of money. This is substantially correct from the practical point of view. But it also presents the view of human beings as rationalists who know what they want and pursue the decision consistently throughout. In this chapter, the question of whose wants is the central theme. In addition to economic ends, we noted that it is important for us to consider the possibilities of students pursuing an education qualification for self-expression and achievement, particular upon reasonable satisfaction of physical and social needs as Abraham Maslow has argued in his famous Hierarchy of Needs Theory.

Students have enormous potential and talent, and it is the responsibility of the institutions to find ways to identify and nurture them. Educators ought to understand what motivates students so that they display curiosity and respond to challenges more enthusiastically and that the students actually learn and want to learn something. In other words, we need to ask—how students learn in the digital age?

"*Market Signalling.*" Spence recognizes that markets are imperfect. Job market being one of them. Information gaps provide an incentive for individuals (job seekers) to find ways to distinguish themselves to gain an advantage over their peers. Investing in education is deemed necessary in his theory to signal high ability and high individual productivity in the labor market. Human Capital Theory and Signaling Theory share some commonalities. Both theories state the individuals would pursue education so long as the benefit of the decision outweighs the cost. Both theories convey the message that education contributes to productivity. Signaling theory can be viewed as an extension of the Human Capital Theory. Andrew Weiss made this point, noting that "sorting models extend human capital theory models by allowing for some productivity differences that firms do not observe to be correlated with the costs or benefits of schooling." Weiss, "*Human Capital Vs. Signaling,*" 134.

CHAPTER 6

Learning in the Digital Age

Our existence depends on our ability to think and learn. We think and by doing so we learn. In fact, humans learn and think throughout our lives. As infants, we learn the world of words. As students, we acquire basic knowledge of the subjects we learn. As adults, we apply what we have learned and learn on the job to earn a living. As elders, we learn from the young when we share our knowledge. It is through continued learning that we acquire analytical skills and the ability to assess problems and apply reasoning. Few people recognize that when hiring companies are looking for the right candidates with a set of skills and credentials, they were looking to hire someone with the passion to learn and the ability to learn; a person who is less interested in being right all the time but is more keen to consider different views learn about them and argue productively about them.

How does the Internet affect our ability to learn? How does the Internet affect student performance? What are the implications to higher education institutions? In this chapter and the following chapter, we set forth to answer these questions.

About the Human Brain

Let us start with the human brain. Study of the functions of the brain is known as neuroscience. One of the brain's functions is learning. Brain activities are complex but increasingly we know more about them.

The brain forms one part of the nervous system. It resembles the head of a cauliflower and has the size of a large grapefruit. A 1.5-kilogram mass of jelly, the brain consists of mostly water (about 78%), fats (10%), and protein (8%). The outer covering, which is the wrinkle part, is the cerebral cortex. It is as thick as an orange peel. The texture is like soft butter although some parts are gooey like jelly and raw eggs.

Scientists have divided the brain into lobes. The occipital lobe, which is located in the middle back area of the brain is primarily responsible for vision. The temporal lobe, which is located above and around the ears on the left and right side of the brain is responsible for hearing, language, and memory. The frontal lobe, which is around the forehead, take control of activities such as judging, creativity, problem solving, and planning. The parietal lobe, which is located on top and back areas of the head is primarily responsible in processing higher sensory and language functions. The middle part of the brain consists of the limbic system, which is responsible for emotions, sleep, attention, hormones, sexuality, sense of smell, and production of brain chemicals.

The structure of the brain is made up of neurons. It is hard to know exactly how many of these nerve cells are there in the brain, possibly in the range of 50 to 100 billion of them. Neurons are the basic units of the brain just like a person is the basic unit of a city. Each neuron is an individual entity. It makes connections, about 1,000 to 10,000 contacts, with other neurons through a small gap between them (the synapse), creating a large number of brain states, and of permutation and combination of brain activities. The neurons have their own agenda without directly communicating with each other. Synapses therefore play an essential role of building the connection with individual neurons using chemical and electrical signals, transferring message and instructions between the neurons, and linking senses to other parts of the nervous system. Neurons are in large measure irrelevant without the synapses.

How Do We Learn?

Our learning ability is dependent on the neurodevelopmental function, the algorithms that influence the strength of the synapses. There are different clusters of neurodevelopmental functions to determine our capability to perform specific skills. The significance of discovering the neurodevelopmental function and network is aptly summarized by Steven Pinker.

> A momentous discover of 20th century theoretical neuroscience is that networks of neurons not only can preserve information but can transform it in ways that allows us to explain how brains can be

intelligent. To input neurons can be connected to an output neuron in such a way that their firing patterns correspond to logical relations such as AND, OR and NOT, or to a statistical decision that depends on the weight of the incoming evidence … It can transform the information about the world that it receives from the sense organs in a way that mirrors the laws governing the world, which in turn allows it to make useful inferences and predictions.[1]

The neurodevelopmental function is individualized, resulting in different abilities and capabilities. There are some who learn better by reading books and articles. Some may prefer to write or take notes or listen to talks or seminars. There are people who learn by doing. Some persons are better in building computers and bridges. Others may be more capable in building planes and road systems. Some may have problems differentiating between left and right, but are perfectly wired to compose songs and symphonies. There are persons who are able to speak a language but are not able to read the same language. Some have difficulty writing even though they have a lot to say. Other individuals may find it challenging to find the exact words they need when they talk.[2]

In the process of learning, we gather information, which comes from the senses. The information is transmitted into what is known as thalamus (in the limbic system) for initial processing. The information is then routed to the relevant structure of the brain for further processing, such as amygdala (which controls human emotions) or hippocampus (which

---

[1] Pinker, *"Enlightened Now,"* p. 21.
[2] While speaking a particular language can be picked up naturally from parents and relatives, reading is not a natural activity for humans or a basic human function. As Maryanne Wolf told us: "We human beings have to learn to read. This means we must have an environment that helps us to develop and connect a complex assortment of basic and not-so-basic processes, so that every young brain can form its own brand-new reading circuit." The same applies to writing. Some of us cannot seem to form letters quickly and accurately enough to keep up with our thoughts and ideas. The written output will appear inferior as compared to their thinking. It is for these reasons that academic reading and writing skills are embedded in the university curriculum to help students cope with the program. See Wolf, *"Reader, Come Home,"* p. 18.

stores the information). The information is filtered, and transferred to short-term memory. We pay attention to the information in the short-term memory so that we will not lose it quickly. Working memory is part of short-term memory, to focus on information longer than short-term memory will permit and allow us to follow instructions and make comparisons. Information is also transferred to long-term memory, which can last a lifetime. Long-term memory is also known as the personal warehouse of permanent knowledge. Your name, address, and date of birth, for example, are stored in the long-term memory.

When it comes to learning, we are often lazy. We rely on processed rules of thumb—heuristics—to help us make decisions. Nobel Laureate Daniel Kahneman and his colleagues have studied decision making of individuals and argued that there are two distinct ways of thinking.[3] System 1 thinking is quick and automatic and imposes little or no effort on the individual. System 1 is emotional and quick thinking. System 2 thinking is effortful, requiring strong mental energy to make a conclusion that is based on real reasoning and logic. System 2 requires the individual to allocate time to sit down and think things through, a luxury that many today are not able to afford in the digital age. Certainly System 1 thinking is crucial. Imagine we try to check everything before making a decision. Time would not have been spent constructively, and the world we live in would be a complete mess. The concern arises when System 1 overtakes everything else, including times when deep thinking is necessary.

Culture also matters in learning. In *Geography of Thought*, Richard Nisbett compares the thinking process of Asians and Westerners.[4] Nisbett argued that Asians think of the world as a circle, paying attention to a wide range of events and searching for relationship between things. As such, in an experiment involving Chinese children to group three items—a chicken, a cow, and the grass—a majority of them would prefer to group the objects on the basis of relationship. In this case, the cow and the grass go together because the cow eats the grass. Asians are also better in learning the meaning of a transitive verb because it involves

---

[3] His work is summarized in the book *Thinking, Fast and Slow*. See Kahneman, "Thinking, Fast and Slow."
[4] Nisbett, "The Geography of Thought."

the relationship between two objects. Nisbett used the example of "to throw" to illustrate the relationship between the use of the arm and the movement of an object through the air.

Westerners, on the other hand, think of the world as a line, focusing on salient objects or things rather than the larger picture. Westerners believe that the behavior of objects is governed by rules. In the experience involving the chicken, the cow, and the grass, American children would express the preference to group objects by taxonomic category—the cow and the children go together as they fit into the animal category. Because categories are denoted by nouns, westerners generally find it easier to learn nouns than verbs. Child-rearing practices in both parts of the world seem to play a role in directing children either more toward relationship in the Asians or more toward categorization of objects in the case of the westerners.

How Does the Internet Affect Our Ability to Learn?

Imagine for a moment how technology has affected our lives. Notice that when planes landed, we can see that the first thing people would do is to switch on their handphones. Handphone and the Internet has become such a necessity. The thought of leaving home without a handphone or entering a premise without Wi-Fi is alarming.

Consider the following statistics, which show the prevalent of technology and Internet usage.

- In the United States, a study found that only 3 out of 220 students were able to turn off their handphones for 72 hours.[5]
- In South Korea, 52 percent of children aged between three and five years old spent on average four hours per week on the Internet.[6] About 72 percent of children owned a smartphone by ages 11 to 12, spending up to 5.4 hours a day on them.[7]

---

[5] Quoted from Watson, "*Future Minds,*" p. 17.
[6] Ibid., p. 28.
[7] Howard, "*When Kids Get Their First Cell Phones Around the World.*"

- Addiction to online game is especially prevalent. About two million South Koreans—nearly 1 in 10 online users—are addicted to the internet.[8]
- In the United Kingdom, 90 percent of children have a handphone by their 11th birthday while 57 percent of them reported that they always sleep with their phone by their bed.[9]
- Oxfam reported that in 2007, 76 percent of the 5- to 15-year olds in the United Kingdom have access to a tablet at home up from 71 percent in 2013. Ninety-two percent of the 5- to 15-year olds go online using any of the digital devices, up from 87 percent in 2013.[10]
- In the United States, the average age for a child getting their first smartphone is 10.3 years. In 2016, 64 percent of kids have access to the Internet via their own laptop or tablet up from just 42 percent in 2012.[11]
- According to a study by Common Sense Media, the U.S. teens on average spent about nine hours a day on the screen for entertainment. Tweens—those between right and 12 years old spent on average six hours a day.[12]
- In Germany, about 51 percent of the children aged between 6 and 13 report having their own mobile phone. Across Europe, about 46 percent of children between the age of 9 and 16 owned a smartphone.[13]
- In Singapore, a person spent on average 12 hours 42 minutes a day on their digital devices such as such as mobile phones, tablets, computers, and video game consoles. Seventy-eight percent of the respondents said that they checked their smartphone or tablet when waking up in the morning.[14]

---

[8] McCurry, "*Internet Addiction Driving South Koreans into Realms of Fantasy.*"
[9] The Guardian, "*Most Children Own Mobile Phone by Age of Seven, Study Finds.*"
[10] Oxfam, "*Children and Parents.*"
[11] Molina, B. "*When Is the Right Age to Buy Your Child a Smartphone?*"
[12] Common Sense Media, "*The Common Sense Media Census.*"
[13] Howard, "*When Kids Get Their First Cell Phones Around the World.*"
[14] Lin and Toh, "*People in Singapore Spend Over 12 Hours on Gadgets Daily: Survey.*"

Indeed, the Internet has led to a proliferation of information and other distractions, most notable online games that is putting tremendous pressure on the human brain especially the working memory. Online activities, data, and information draw out mental energy and attention, dividing them thinly across the various demand and affecting our problem-solving capability. When the load of information exceeds the capacity of the working memory, cognitive load is resulted. When this happens, we are not able to retain information nor draw inference with the information that is already stored in the long-term memory.

Eric Schmidt, the former CEO and Chairman of Google, has expressed worry that the level of interruption caused by social media and digital contents is affecting our ability to engage in deep learning. "The sort of overwhelming rapidity of information … is in fact affecting cognition. It is affecting deep thinking. I still believe that sitting down and reading a book is the best way to really learn something. And I worry that we are losing that."[15] Reading a book while doing a crossword puzzle, Nicholas Carr wrote, is "the intellectual environment of the Internet." Such intensive exercise can "impede deep learning and thinking."[16]

---

[15] Quoted in Greenfield, *"Mind Change,"* p. 27.
[16] Carr, *"The Shallows,"* *126.* For deep learning to occur, learning must be made relevant to the learner. Having prior knowledge of the subject is necessary. Hirsch, E.D. has written extensively on the relevance of prior knowledge. He wrote; "Leaning is cumulative, and at first it is slow. Knowledge gradually builds on knowledge; the principle behind intellectual capital is that it takes knowledge to make knowledge. Because of the cumulative character of learning, the educational conditions of early life exercise a very powerful influence on later competencies. Small early deficits tend to become large deficiencies in later life; small initial advantages tend to grow into large ones later." He also noted that "the cumulative effects of intellectual capital derive from there being at least two learning advantages in possessing relevant background knowledge. The first advantage is that there are fewer things which have to be learned," minimizing errors and retrys. The second advantage "in possessing lots of intellectual capital; the broader the base of relevant knowledge, the greater the number of potential analogies or categories available for assimilating new learnings. This increase in cognitive hooks gives educated adults a learning advantage over young children, who, in raw processing ability, may far outshine them." See Hirsch, *"The Schools We Need and Why We Don't Have Them,"* pp. 225–226. Critically, Hirsch cited the Thomas

Technological impact on reading and learning is not a new phenomenon. Concerns, for example, arose when written form of language was invented to give way to reading as the way to learn and transfer knowledge. The great philosopher Socrates was against the reading way of learning, noting that it could implant forgetfulness in their souls and ultimately the death of memory. Through his student Plato, we were warned that written ideas had the "potential to acquire life of their own." As Frank Furedi said "Socrates asserted that writing is indiscriminate in that 'it roams about everywhere'; it does not discern between readers who can understand and benefit from its communication, and those will become misled and confused by it."[17] Socrates in this regard belongs to the group of oral masters that includes Buddha and Jesus Christ. To them, the text read was nothing but its words.

Sticht's Law that provides a useful oracy-to-literacy approach, an indication of what is necessary to enable deep learning to take place. For nondeaf persons, the law states that:
- comprehension of written languages cannot exceed the comprehension of oral language
- reading ability cannot exceed listening ability
- oral speech is the foundation of written speech

[17] Furedi, "*Power of Reading*," p. 3. Yet, as Furedi remarked "the very manner in which this condemnation (on technology of writing) was communicated—through a written text (by Plato)—indicated that even its author could not reject literacy in its entirety" (ibid., p. 13). Senaca, a philosopher, had similarly raised the concern about reading. Reading too many books could cause "distraction" and tend to make the readers 'discursive and unsteady (ibid., p. 143). Others like Edmund Burke had regarded printing and reading as problematic because learning was no longer situated in a proper place such as the institution of learning thereby subjecting the read to moral corrupting effect. There was the fear that "you become what you read" (ibid., p. 104). If reading is about translating and deciphering signs and symbols, any misinterpretation and disassociation has to be resulted from the reader, and not from the texts. When reading, it is common to miss the main ideas or be confused between the main ideas and minor points. The reader may also fail to establish the connection between the points or messages raised by the author or extract the key themes or arguments or understand the words or concepts used by the authors and so missing the meaning of sections in the texts.

The invention of writing and movable type printing in Europe by Johannes Gutenberg around 1440 led to a surge in the number of printed materials, and further changed the way people acquire information and transmit knowledge.[18] Before printing, only a few thousand books were in circulation in Europe. The job of producing a book then was simply too massive. Fifty years after printing was introduced, the number of books had risen to more than 900,000. Ideas were shared and more knew about them.

There are so many books printed today that in one's lifetime, we can possibly read only a tiny fraction of the total. As Zaid Gabriel noted, a full-time reader can probably read four books a week or 200 titles a year and 10,000 books over 50 years, which compared to over 50 million books in existence, represents only a small proportion of the collective output of books.[19] The response from readers and students is not about the number of books that they have read. Rather it should be about the applicability of the contents read that the readers can usefully adopt in their workplace and life.

The introduction of the printing press and communications technology is revolutionary in the sense that they do not add or subtract something; they have changed everything. Neil Postman wrote: "In the year 1500, fifty years after the printing press was invented, we did not have old Europe plus the printing press. We have a different Europe."[20] Similarly, with the Internet, the world has not become the world plus the Internet. It has led to a new world. Because of the impact, it is only logical that the new technology is subject to strict scrutiny, harsh comments, and rejection.

---

[18] An engraver and a gem-cutter, Gutenberg realized that if the alphabet letters could be cut in the form of reusable type rather than as wooden block, printing could be done much faster and efficiently. Gutenberg's invention led to the print revolution, from books to journals, newspapers, memos and magazines. Between 1450 and 1455, Gutenberg produced a bible with 42 lines to each page. The book was the first book printed on type.

[19] Gabriel, "*So Many Books*," p. 24.

[20] Postman, "*Technopoly*," p. 18.

In a series of path-breaking essays and publications, most notably *Understanding Media,* Marshall McLuhan argued that technology was not merely a neutral conduit but itself would have an impact on the mental process of the users—"the medium is the message." The technology—print, television, and electronic communication—can have a distorting effect on human's ability to think imaginatively and consciously. Teachers and schools assigning reading materials, to take an example, are encouraging students to read other people's thought and forming a homogenous culture. McLuhan's preference is to encourage students to think on their own and convey their own thoughts—to be "differentiated, not by their specialist skills or visible marks, but by their unique emotional mixes."[21]

When books got printed in large quantity, many were concerned about information overload. Many still are concerned about infobesity. We have created technologies to store and transmit information. But our bodies and minds still operate at the same tempo as they did in the ancient. We still have two eyes and two ears. We can hardly engage in constructive conversation with two or more persons at the same time. Digitalization gets rid of all the friction, speeding things up but taxes our power of concentration and attention. There are consequences with too much information. Notably, diversity of publications raised questions about the readers' ability to differentiate between authoritative information and those that

---

[21] McLuhan, "*Understanding Media,*" p. 50. Prior to McLuhan's critic, there were others who have attacked printing for distracting us, undermining thinking and affecting the readers capacity to reflect. In the 18th century, traditionalists such as English Romantic poet William Wordsworth (1770–1850) was concerned about the spread of rapid and superficial reading as a large number of readers turned to popular culture such as novels. Elites feared that reading could lead to ideological challenges and rebellion from educated peasant. Interestingly, the proliferation of readings contents on the Internet has produced similar fear, like the printing press, to transmit "unhealthy information and influence the minds of readers." Some have remarked that McLuhan's writings had supported users of the Internet, with its active online community serving as a platform for mankind to return to the pre-Gutenbergian way of life. Furedi quoted Lewis Laphan's explanation in the Introduction of McLuhan's Understanding Media. In his essay, Laphan wrote that "McLuhan believes that the unifying networks of electronic communication might restore mankind to a state of bliss not unlike the one said to have existed within the Garden of Eden." Furedi, "*Power of Reading,*" p. 189.

contain fake and distorting views.[22] Readers speed read, affecting their capacity to digest and reflect on what was read. Because knowledge and information shared over the Internet are so easily accessible, we suffer from "knowledge illusion"—allowing others to do the thinking for us. This happens because it is difficult to reject the opinion shared by Internet users especially when we do not know for sure what is true or fake. Our beliefs and knowledge enmesh with that of others.[23] Too much information has also caused employees to make mistakes. Satya Chakravorty studied aircraft manufacturing and repair companies and discovered that they created information overload for their factory workers. Besides dealing with daily operational matters, the workers faced hundreds of pages of training materials to review, creating "brain overload." The workers were overwhelmed and started to make silly mistakes.[24]

How Does the Internet Affect Student Performance?

Studies have shown that the amount of time spent on the social media has a negative effect on grade point average score. Anne Margen and her colleagues conducted a study to compare the performance of paper readers and those who read on the screen.[25] They found that electronic readers performed poorly in comprehension. Hanho Jeong, from Chongshin University, Seoul, conducted a similar study on sixth-year school students. Again, electronic readers have poorer comprehension skills. In addition, the author found significantly greater eye fatigue among the electronic readers.[26]

---

[22] On the concerns about information overload resulted from the growth in printed materials, see Ann Blair's "*Too Much to Know.*" Blair explained that the problem of overabundance was raised as early as the mid-16th century. Equally concerning was the difficulty in reconciling conflicting views arising from the printed materials.

[23] Sloman and Fernbach, "*The Knowledge Illusion,*" p. 16.

[24] Chakravorty, "*The Trouble With Too Much Information.*"

[25] Mangen, Walgermo and Bronnick, "*Reading Linear Texts on Paper Versus Computer Screen.*"

[26] Jeong, "*A Comparison of The Influence of Electronic Books and Paper Books on Reading Comprehension, Eye Fatigue, and Perception.*"

Higher education requires students to think hard—to learn and apply difficult concepts and solve challenging and unfamiliar problems, the hardest work there is as Henry Ford told us. It deals with abstract rather than concrete, using qualifications such as "assuming that," "unless" and equivalent, and requires the transfer of memory from long-term memory to working memory. To think effectively, a person needs sufficient room in the working memory. But human's working memory is limited in capacity. The working memory bank needs to rest and recharge. Without adequate rest, our attention lifespan and the ability to learn is adversely affected. Students today however are so occupied with their digital devices and staying up at night on the Internet that they barely have enough time to rest. Many feel tired at school due to the lack of rest. Lee Hyang-woon, a neurologist at Ewha Womans University Medical Center, has linked extensive use of the technology to sleep disorder. "The greater the intensity of light from smartphone screens, and the longer you are exposed to it, the more likely you will experience sleep disturbance and reduced quality of sleep."[27] Furthermore, students are forced to do things as fast as possible. They have to think fast, write quickly, meet submission deadlines, comprehend, solve problems, calculate, remember on the spot, and complete x number of questions in quizzes and examinations within a tight time frame. These impose tremendous pressure on the brain.

That is why when schoolwork is too onerous and difficult, the students struggle and would not like school much; to avoid thinking. That is why students find their higher education journey challenging—to make sense of the theories and terminologies associated with the subjects.[28]

Corner cutting is prevalent amongst the learners. They skim the contents and appear to be in a hurry to complete the reading. They read at the surface and very quickly, too fast to comprehend at a deeper level. It is of course not uncommon for a reader to find difficulty comprehending the contents. In the past, what one would do is to go back and reread the article, passage, and so on. But students today are less patient. They have

---

[27] Arin, *"Too Much Time on Smartphone Poses Health Threat."*
[28] Some may say that this is a deliberate part of higher education; to build the sophistication and resilience in students and ultimately to engage in higher levels of thinking.

a wide range of things that they can do with their digital devices—managing their social media accounts, taking photos, playing online games, watching and making videos, and so on.

Reading online is often distracted by hypertexts.[29] In 2001, Canadian scholars asked 70 persons to read a short story. The participants were divided into two group: one group read the story in a traditional manner and the second group read the story with links as we would find on the Internet. It was found that the second group of readers took a longer time to read the story, and yet more of them reported the inability to understand the story. They were more confused about what they read as compared to the first group. Hypertext readers often could not remember what had and had not read.[30]

In electronic reading, readers develop the "grasshopper mind," hopping from point to point.[31] They get distracted by the hypertexts and detour from the path of linear thought, therefore affecting comprehension. "Evaluating links and navigating a path through them (hypertexts)," wrote Nicholas Carr, "involves mentally demanding problem-solving tasks that are extraneous to the act of reading itself. Deciphering hypertext substantially increases readers' cognitive load and hence weakens their ability to comprehend and retain that they're reading."[32]

Even avid readers are not spared. Susan Blum, a cultural, linguistic, and psychological anthropologist at University of Notre Dame has said that she could not concentrate on reading as much as she used to do with all the digital devises, applications and contents.[33] Maryanne Wolf, author of bestsellers *Readers, Come Home* and *Proust and the Squid* admitted that the way she read has changed over the years. "I now read on the surface and very quickly," she writes, "I read too fast to comprehend

---

[29] Some have argued that hypertexts are useful to allow readers to make connections among diverse but related texts thereby exposing the readers to various or alternative viewpoints.

[30] For details, see Carr, *"The Shallows: What the Internet Is Doing to Our Brains,"* p. 127.

[31] See Wiegel and Gardner, *"The Best of Both Literacies."*

[32] Carr, *"The Shallows: What the Internet Is Doing to Our Brains,"* p. 126.

[33] See Blum, *"'I Love Learning. I Hate School': An Anthropology of College."*

deeper levels, which forced me constantly to go back and reread the same sentence over and over with increasing frustration."[34] Imagine those who are less devoted to reading.

Notably, reading on the Internet is different. Research conducted by Liu Ziming, a professor at San Jose State University who tracked eye movement found that web users hardly followed a line-by-line way of reading (the "E" style). A vast majority of the respondents skimmed the text quickly, and skipped lines as they went along, resembling the letters "F" or "T." The eyes would move so quickly across the screen that one could only wonder if the article was read at all or with a zig-zag style, with some reading on the first few lines of the screen, then a little in the middle and a few lines at the end.[35] The lack of "cognitive patience" has an adverse effect on critical analysis in the deep-reading circuit, which demand patience, time, and effort.

These distracting technologies have the tendency of lowering the level of concentration of students both inside and outside of the classroom. The Internet and the smartphone provide for multitasking behaviors motivated by connection, addition, and massive amount of entertainment contents. Multitasking—reading online news, listening to music, and playing online games with the same devise—imposes pressure on the brain. Each time we work on a different task, the brain has to reorient itself, adding to our cognitive load, affecting our comprehension, and increasing the likelihood of missing important information and misinterpreting the contents of what we have read.

Maryanne Wolf has argued that the cognitive threat of digital based culture is real and disturbing. Readers today are "hyperattentive," bombarded with "sensory stimuli" across multiple digital channels. Wolf noted that on average, an individual checks his or her phone between 150 and 190 times a day.[36] Students are preoccupied with digital contents—e-mails, blogs, text messages, social media contents, and are pretty much exhausted from playing online games. The traditional

---

[34] Wolf, "*Reader, Come Home: The Reading Brain in a Digital World,*" p. 100.
[35] See Liu "*Reading Behaviour in the Digital Environment: Changes in Reading Behaviour Over the Past Ten Years*"; Liu, "*Digital Reading.*"
[36] Wolf, "*Reader, Come Home,*" p. 109.

understanding of learning—being attentive and taking notes in lectures, asking lecturers when in doubt, reading the prescribed textbooks and materials, debating—is under assault. Instead, students learn by "patchwriting" or "copying from a source text, and then deleting some words, altering grammatical structure or plugging in one synonym for another."[37] Plagiarism and cutting corners strike many students as a logical way to accomplish the mission in college given the time constraint especially for students who have no love for learning and are busy with other activities and obligations. The Internet, digital devices, and computer software have made copying easy and tempting.

Implications for Higher Education

Digitization, like globalization, is here to stay. The challenge is not about choosing between printed and online but to find a way to blend the two mediums to ensure the best learning outcomes for our students.[38] It is about finding ways to cope with technology and deal with its challenges so that our education system continues to do its job of imparting useful knowledge and skills to students.

Today's learners are exposed to Internet-based information retrieval and InfoComm technology is an integral part of their social life. Learning through information retrieval from the web since their first "Google" search has deeply reinforced the role of information navigation in their learning development. To this end, discovery-based learning, an approach which puts learners in control of their learning with hands-on exploration, applying inquiry processes, peer reinforcement of factual information and concepts, has been trending in the digital age. Learning through unique experiences and through Discovery-Based Learning first proposed

---

[37] Howard, "*Standing in the Shadow of Giants*," p. xvii.
[38] There are certainly positive aspects of the Internet. Children and students today get the benefit of not just what their parents, grandparents or great parents know. They get the benefit of what everybody else in the world knew in the years in school and thereafter. Internet has allowed learners to receive feedback from their teachers very quickly, including assessment marks that are graded by the system. It is amazing that there are many people in the world today who are, with good intention, willing to share their knowledge and communicate.

by Jerome Bruner in the 1960s have re-emerged as a hybrid learning trend in the digital age along with constructivism learning.[39] Modern classroom instruction has moved swiftly to integrate elements of discovery-based learning to enhance learning competency and critical skills development.[40]

Susan Blum has observed that students in her class lacked the attention and ability to absorb information.[41] Her students did not usually buy the prescribed textbooks, preferring shorter and accessible texts (rather than the original version). She believed that this would pose a challenge to lecturers, particularly those who steadfastly abide to assigning classic texts in the original version to their students. An avid reader herself, Blum is of the opinion that it is unimaginable to give up computers and the Internet and return to read the physical books. And with that, reading would change too. As educators who do the writing, she feels that they should adapt to the changing environment and get the writing that suits the time and era. One can deduce that electronic reading is more suited to acquiring factual knowledge and short pieces whereas reading on paper is more suitable to allow one to understand abstract concepts and overall argument.

Maryanne Wolf shares the same sentiment. She made it clear that she is "less interested in the degree of difference between our digitally raised children and ourselves than in an understanding of what is best for children's development regardless of the milieu and, in particular, within this exponentially changing milieu. There is no going back, and with some historical digression aside, there almost never has been."[42] She suggests constructing a biliterate mind in our students, which is steeped in both traditional and digital mediums of communications. It is useful for students to be able to learn to think in each medium, and develop and internalize the particular characteristics of the two mediums. Wolf illustrates with the example of a student who combines reading of stories

---

[39] Ozdem-Yilmaz and Bilican, "*Discovery Learning—Jerome Bruner.*"
[40] See Herlily, Anhar, Ahda, and Sumarmin, "*Application of Learning Model Learning Guided Discovery With Scientific Approach to Enhance Learning Competency Science Seventh Grade Students.*"
[41] Blum, "*I Love Learning. I Hate School.*"
[42] Wolf, "*Reader, Come Home,*" p. 106.

and discussing about refugee children with online access to actual footage of migrant refugee children as one effective way to tap on both mediums to improve learning capacity.

The Internet can be a powerful tool to supplement traditional learning if it is used constructively. Databases, case studies and trusted online articles can be tailored to student needs with asynchronous sessions to allow students to learn at their own pace. With the Internet, students can gain access to a wide social network to learn from peers and keep the momentum of learning. The experiences that students gain through online learning and networking are comparable to how organizations operate in the global economy—in decision making and communication with stakeholders, for example—thereby providing the necessary training to students before they enter the labor force. It is imperative for higher education institutions to embrace the use of technology and the Internet; to combine technology with traditional educational delivery to drive personalized learning, to develop new content and resources available through the Internet and offer a curriculum that is more flexible, more adaptive, and more responsive to the needs of the students.

Teachers matter and are great change agents to shape a learner beyond just imparting bodies of knowledge. Great teachers guide their students to adjust and adapt to an ever-changing globalized society and realize their potential in the digital world. Teachers can help students to use technology in appropriate ways. Technology has been perceived to be the key driver to transform teaching by ushering in a new model of technology-enabled, engaged, and active learning classroom environment.[43] Popular technology tools like Kahoot and Mentimeter have been deployed successfully to support and supplement teaching and learning, identify weaker students and gauge students' understanding of the subject contents. Teachers can design assessments that allow students to use digital cameras to take photos, make videos and collaborate with other students to make the lessons more relevant and fun. More importantly, the teacher's impact on students should go beyond grades. Students need to be imparted with digital navigation skills, which includes finding information, assessing the

---

[43] Prestridge and De Aldama, "*A Classification Framework for Exploring Technology-Enabled Practice.*"

reliability[44] of the information and prioritizing information to discern the limits of technology and promote self-learning and lifelong learning. By embracing technology and the Internet, teachers can turn students from passive receivers of information to active thinkers.

It is about accepting the technology and recognizing the growing use of the Internet in student's everyday life. It is about seeking to understand and being empathetic with students' feelings in the digital age. Carl Roger's work on psychotherapy is instrumental in this regard. To facilitate the growth potential of passionate learners, teachers need to first cultivate a genuine relationship with the students, that is, teachers have to be recognized as being trustworthy and dependably real. "To the extent that the teacher creates such a relationship with his class, student will become a self-initiated learner, more original, more self-disciplined, less anxious, and other-directed."[45] It is important for teachers to accept students for who they are, no matter what their conditions, behaviors and feelings are, and to "respect and liking" for the student as a separate person and "a willingness for him to possess his own feelings in his own way."[46] Finally, teachers must attempt to understand their students, and not make immediate evaluation and judgment about the students. By seeking to understand, Rogers argued that students would be more open to communicate their feelings. It is about being emphatic with the student feelings to "enter fully into the world of his feelings" and "see his private world through his eyes."[47]

The problem with some of the schools today is that they are merely factories producing unthinking students. This is dangerous particularly in the age where there are so much unverified information circulating around the Internet. Teachers should have the skill in the art and science to plant doubts into the students' mind, to create strong interest to read and encourage students to ask why. Teaching is not only about

---

[44] This point was brought up by respondents in the Thought Leadership Programme developed in partnership by Corsham Institute and RAND Europe. See RAND, "*Digital Leaning.*"
[45] Rogers, "*On Becoming a Person,*" p. 37.
[46] Ibid., p. 34.
[47] Ibid., p. 34.

knowledge acquisition. It is also about fundamentally transform students to question the status quo. If teachers can teach students to articulate their ideas clearly in their words and in writing, stand for their rights to speak up and expand their pool of knowledge, education can make them better citizens.

CHAPTER 7

Good to Great Teachers

What do teachers do? Quite a lot apparently. They are responsible for delivering the subject contents, inform students of the subject requirements, map out the critical concepts, and help students plan their learning journey. Imparting soft skills like critical thinking and judgment, problem solving, teamwork, and personal resilience is important in the digital age, so are traditional roles of teachers like improving students' speaking, writing, and reading skills.

Teachers serve as role models of good behavior and are expected to treat their students fairly and professionally. Great teachers are aware that they already know the subject matter whereas the students are only learning. A great teacher responds to poor understanding of concepts and subject contents by focusing and explaining the concepts and topics again, recognizing that some learners are slower and less prepared than others, and will require more attention from them.

Teachers almost always teach solo, out of sight of others. They have no witnesses other than the students. Some blame themselves for failing, without really knowing why. Psychologists David Burns who taught at Stanford University School of Medicine has shown that a lot of bad feeling and negativity are based on thinking errors such as labelling oneself as a failure, leading to depression and other emotional problems. Teachers develop bad feelings because students were not attentive in class and the class records a low passing rate. Teachers need to learn to deal with criticisms that can be exaggerated and inaccurate. Burns has devised a useful technique for teachers to deal with students who are intensely critical of the materials presented in class; to "silence such a person in an inoffensive manner." The technique involves the following four steps: (i) immediately thank the person for his or her comments, (ii) acknowledge that the points brought by the students are indeed important, (iii) emphasize that there is a need for more knowledge about the points raised, encourage the student to "pursue meaningful research and investigation of the topic," and (iv) invite the student to share his or her views following the end of the session.[1]

Undoubtedly, some students can be hard to teach. They are silent, withdrawn; they have little interest nor the capacity for conversation; they have short attention span, dislike engaging with ideas and friends; they have no directions and lack motivation. The problem is especially worrying today. Jean Twenge, in her book *iGen: Why Today's Super-Connected Kids Are Growing Up Less Rebellious, More Tolerant and Less Happy—And Completely Unprepared for Adulthood*, focused on the generation she called 'iGen—kids who were born between 1995 and 2012, the first generation of kids who entered adolescence with smartphones in their hands. She concluded that this group of people is on the brink of the worst mental health crisis in decades with rising rates of teen depression and suicide since 2011. And this is due mainly to extensive use of smartphones.[2] In her article *How Smartphones Destroyed a Generation,* she commented that "the arrival of smartphone has practically changed every aspect of teenagers' lives, from the nature of their social interaction to their mental health."[3]

Teaching is therefore a challenging yet noble work. Teachers feel the pressure to cover the syllabus within a tight schedule and constantly at fear of losing their job because of poor evaluation scores from students. Despite the challenges, the teaching profession has continuously been attracting members into its ranks. Satisfaction of seeing learners advance and achieve their potential under their guidance reinforces this as a unique career choice.[4]

---

[1] Students may find the steps useful as well in dealing with emotional health problems. See Burns, "*Feeling Good.*"
[2] Twenge, "*iGen.*" iGen refers to individual who were born in 1995 and later. The Internet was commercialized in 1995. Many in the iGen would not remember a time before the Internet. The older members of iGen would be around 12 years old when iPhone introduced in 2007 and would have entered high school when iPad was introduced in 2010.
[3] Twenge, "*How Smartphones Destroyed a Generation.*"
[4] Priyadharshini and Robinson-Pant, "*The Attractions of Teaching.*"

Teachers and their actions certainly matter. It can be as simple as showing up in class to provide a certain amount of order and routine. After all, students have limited working memory. It is more effective and efficient to have teachers facilitate learning and demonstrate through worked examples how to solve a problem than to have students discover the solution through trial and error without many instructions.

In the digital age, teachers guide learners to access reliable online information and think of ways to utilize technology and online tools to supplement classroom teaching. Online games, for example, can be constructively used to encourage discovery, perseverance, communication, and collaboration in multiplayer settings. This chapter shall examine teaching methods and strategies teachers should know.

What Makes a Good Teacher Great?

- Motivate, Not Label Your Students and Give Purposeful Feedback

Many educators consider motivation as a crucial factor that promotes students' engagement and consequently their performances in learning. Motivated students are attentive in class, and in general, studies have established positive relationships between students' motivation and performances.[5] In *The Courage to Teach,* Parker Palmer notes that students who lack the motivation to study, want to "find their voices, speak their voices, have their voices heard." A great teacher in this case is someone who will "listen to those voices even before they are spoken—so that someday they can speak with truth and confidence." What does it mean by listening to a voice before it is spoken? Palmer explains: "It means not rushing to fill our students' silences with fearful speech of our own and not trying to coerce them into saying the things that we want to hear. It means entering empathetically into the student's world so that he or

---

[5] See Pavlou, "*Pre-adolescents' Perceptions of Competence, Motivation and Engagement in Art Activities*"; Pintrich, "*A Motivational Science Perspective on the Role of Student Motivation in Learning and Teaching Contexts.*"

she perceives you as someone who has the promise of being able to hear another person's truth."[6]

A great teacher refrains from labelling students as lazy, troublemaker, useless, weak, and unmotivated. He understands that some of the students treat poor performance in education with humiliation, receiving labels that can somehow be permanent. A great teacher provides the emotional support and face-to-face guidance to students in the face of frustration, a role that cannot be performed by machines.

If the students fail to submit or complete their work assigned to them, the teacher could tell them with authority that they must submit. The students might submit the work but learn nothing. A great teacher will try a different approach. He would ask if the students needed help or arrange additional lessons to explain the requirements of the assignment or suggest that they submit the work for marking to meet the graduation requirements of the program. The latter approach will increase compliance with less resentment and emotional baggage.

With regard to giving feedback, Virtual Learning Environments (VLEs) such as Canvas, Moodle, and Blackboard can be used to provide individualized and generic comments. For written assignments, VLEs offer a useful platform to provide feedback and comments on individual work or generic feedback that can be posted in the chat group function for all students taking the module to read.

A great teacher understands that feedback to students have to be constructive and purposeful. The teacher does not assume that learners read and care about the comments and will do something about them to avoid making the same mistakes nor assume that students understand the topic well enough to make sense of the sparse feedback and use them effectively. A great teacher explores peer and self-assessment; where students evaluate one another's work or self-evaluate using a well-constructed rubric and take the initiative to speak to students about their work to allow students to seek clarification.

- Identify Students Who Are Weak Early in the Course

---

[6] Palmer, "*The Courage to Teach*," p. 47.

A great teacher knows that students are not alike. Some are better in Mathematics whereas others are more competent in comprehending theoretical concepts. Some students could read well whereas others may find it challenging putting words together to form proper sentences. Knowing what works and where attention is needed help teachers to adjust the pace of teaching and reinforce concepts. A great teacher identifies and helps students who are weak in their studies early in the course and redeems the students all of whom possess remarkable strengths waiting to be untapped. That means as teachers, they keep things in check and make the critical adjustments. Technological tools like Kahoot and Mentimeter can be effectively used to assess understanding of subject contents. Struggling students feel a sense of relief when they know there is help.

- Know What to Teach

Neil Postman writes that great teachers should teach subjects they are weak at in school. If he is weak in Science, teach Science. If the teacher is weak in Mathematics, go ahead and teach Mathematics. This way, the teacher is more likely to understand the struggles faced by the students and offer useful advice and tips to address the challenges. He gets rid of the textbooks that are badly written and has the courage to get students to detect errors made by him. A great teacher gets the students to discover, said Postman. "In this way, … teachers become less interested in making students smart, more interested in making students less dumb."[7]

Adam Grant told the story of the great philosopher Robert Nozick who insisted in teaching a new subject every year on philosophy, neuroscience, religion, thinking about thinking, and Russian Revolution. It seems that Nozick had never taught a subject a second time in his four decades of teaching except once. He explained "Presenting a completely polished and worked out view doesn't give students a feel for what it's like to do original work in philosophy and to see it happen, to catch on to doing it." Nozick's approach was inspiring, wrote Grant, for he (Nozick) was not content for students to learn from him. Rather, he wanted the

---

[7] Postman, "*The End of Education*," p. 114.

students to learn with him. Indeed, "a remarkable model for changing up our familiar methods of teaching—and learning."[8]

- Explore a Variety of Teaching Methods

A great teacher understands that students' behavior and attitude toward education and learning can be culturally based.

For example, education institutions in the Western countries measure understanding by students' ability to vocalize and respond verbally to questions posed in class. They equip speaking with knowledge. To Asians, failure to speak does not mean failure to understand the materials. Speaking is not the fundamental way of understanding the subject. Quoting Lao-Tze, the sixth-century sage who said "How who knows does not speak, he who speaks does not know," Richard Nisbett acknowledged that "there is certainly a long tradition in the East of equating silence rather than speech with knowledge."[9] Students utilize a broad range of stimuli to enhance understanding.

There is therefore no one size fits all approach in teaching. Associating a particular mean of communication to represent and intelligence must be discouraged. Western educators who teach Asian students in the same way as they teach the Western students and complain about the learning attitude of Asian students are barking at the wrong tree.

Consider another example. Academic writing can be perceived differently among Asian students. Typically, in academic writing, students need to respond to a research question. Data is collected, and hypotheses are tested. Conclusions are then drawn from the analysis. Logical rules are applied. Generally speaking, Asians are less accustomed to applying logical rules to events as they are more prone to associate with established beliefs.[10] As a result, they entertain "the plausibility of conclusions" and

---

[8] Grant, "*Think Again*," p. 195.
[9] Nisbett, "*The Geography of Thought*," p. 211.
[10] The Chinese language, with ideographs in place, is one of the most difficult languages to learn. Every stroke counts. Its difficulty, explained former Prime Minister of Singapore Lee Kuan Yew, was meant "to leave ordinary people illiterate and in awe of the Mandarins." Mass education was therefore hindered, which

are in favor of the "desirability of conclusions."[11] Asians would find rhetoric of writing scientific papers a particularly painful process.

In contrast, debate is more common in the West where rhetoric is constructed bit by bit from nursery school through college. Hence, by the time they are graduate students, it is second nature. As a result, as Nisbett argued, "it is not uncommon for American science professors to be impressed by their hard-working, highly selected Asian students and then to be disappointed by their first major paper—not because of their incomplete command of English, but because of their lack of mastery of the rhetoric common in the professor's field."[12] The danger of this is that failure by teachers to recognize the cultural aspect of things can result in low grades awarded to Asians, not necessarily due to lack of comprehension of the subject matter but the lack of Western rhetoric style.

The need to adapt was evident in the wake of the coronavirus outbreak. In-person classes have been cancelled. Teachers have to conduct their lessons online and assess the students through other means to ensure that learning could continue. This poses a challenge—the courses were not designed for online delivery.

To proceed with remote online assessments, teachers are compelled to review the nature of the assignment—randomization of questions, submission through anti-plagiarism software like Turnitin that allow similarity checks—and determine whether students were to attempt the questions and key in directly into the Learning Management System (LMS) or key in the answers elsewhere and upon completion, upload the document into the LMS. Considerations also have to put in place on the use of appropriate media platform for oral viva/speaking examination

---

affected China's advancement in the technological space and innovativeness in the past. Despite the fact that the language has been simplified, the learning of the Chinese language requires an astonishing degree of memory power but "discouraged the faculty of logical and analytical thought, which has become such a firm tradition in the West since Greek and Roman times." See Josey, "*Lee Kuan Yew*," pp. 554, 612.

[11] Nisbett, "*The Geography of Thought*," p. 171.

[12] In contrast Americans are "more in the habit of applying logical rules to ordinary events… and are therefore more capable of ignoring the plausibility of conclusions." Ibid., p. 170.

and any other assessments that require oral presentations. On the LMS, teachers have to consider if back-track is allowed so that students can reattempt the online questions and if online assessments are to be set with time constraint so as to mitigate students from finding answers on the Internet or sharing questions and answers with one another. Teachers have to think about the duration of online assessment, factoring in disruptions resulted from poor Internet connectivity, user ID and password log-in, and upload of answer to the respective platforms' issues and catering to students from different time zones.

It is not uncommon for teachers to struggle in online teaching at least in the initial stage. Some faculty replicate how they taught before COVID-19 hit when they deliver the same modules online. Online teaching is new to most of us so there is no prior knowledge nor experience to rely on. Some of the challenges in conducting online lessons include lack of human contact and collaborative engagement with students, sense of uncertainty if students have grasped contents of the subject, and difficulty in creating mathematical expressions and equations via the LMS. Faculty members might have incorrectly assumed that their students would behave in a similar manner in the online learning environment—staying in class the whole time, taking notes, and learning. But of course, none of these behaviors can remain the same under new and often challenging circumstances. High student absenteeism and less student work completion are not uncommon in all-remote teaching and learning environments.

Undoubtedly, teachers have to learn to deliver effective online lessons, using strategies and techniques such as developing bite-size lectures, utilizing chat-box function on LMS to encourage students to pose questions, delivering interactive lessons to capture the interest of the students, using analogies to make the contents easier for students to understand, encouraging group learning amongst students to build their confidence, and using interactive displays and tablets to display mathematical expressions and equations.

COVID-19 has created a chain reaction on digital innovation, possibly creating a new normal in learning. In the Ipsos survey conducted for the World Economic Forum and published in November 2020, 72 percent of the respondents felt that higher education would be conducted at least as much online as in-person over the next five years. About a quarter of the respondents believed that higher education would be conducted entirely online.[13] In Singapore, the Ministry of Education likewise would integrate blended learning into the national curriculum. By the end of 2022, secondary schools and junior colleges would implement blended Learning at all levels.[14]

The adoption of online learning would not be possible without the teachers' ability and willingness to adapt. Indeed, their participation in the design of the curriculum and assessments and continued learning from one another and adaptability to online teaching will be critical as online learning becomes a new normal.

- Don't Provide Ready Made Solutions

Purely regurgitating concepts and theories from the texts is likely to create discontentment among students. Rote learning for the sake to drilling formulas, conceptual, and theoretical materials into students' minds should be avoided. However, this should not be confused with the necessity to acquire fundamental facts relevant to the field of study. There are certain fundamentals knowledge that are worth memorizing.[15]

What teachers need to avoid is providing ready-made solutions to their students. Students should be encouraged to think of the solutions themselves, applying the knowledge and skills they have acquired in the school and basing their solutions on contextual backgrounds. The challenge to schools is to establish the necessary conditions to encourage the conversion of known ideas to solve unknown and unfamiliar problems. If students learn things from books simply for the sake of reciting what he has learned when called upon, then knowledge in itself is little used outside of the school.

---

[13] IPSOS, "*Higher Education.*"
[14] Ministry of Education, Singapore, "*Blended Learning to Enhance Schooling Experience and Further Develop Students into Self-Directed Learners.*"
[15] Ken Robinson reminded us that there are only 45 words in the First Amendment, which cannot possibly be damaging to the brain to learn them by heart. Robinson and Aronica, "*You, Your Child and School,*" p. 131.

Technology and the Internet can be surprisingly helpful in this regard. Teachers can build activities that encourage students to interact and cocreate with peers locally and from around the world to examine domestic and global issues that interest them, using multidisciplinary resources from the Internet and camera and video functions on their smartphones so that they can share documents, photos, and videos over long distances with minimal loss of information.

- Teach Students How to Learn

Often students find the lessons boring or struggle to complete assignment tasks or passing the subject because they do not know how to learn. We need teachers, great teachers, to teach students how to learn to make learning more effective.[16]

In his famous book *Emile,* Jean-Jacques Rousseau begins on the premise that humans by nature are good. Education helps to cultivate the goodness in us to engage the society and relate to follow citizens in the natural way. The appropriate way to do is to make the students curious to comprehend things themselves. "If he makes mistakes, let him do it; do not correct the errors, but wait in silence till he is in a condition to see them and to correct them for himself; or at most, on a favourable occasion introduce some procedure which will make him conscious of them," wrote Rousseau.[17] The role of an educator in this regard is to teach students how to learn, and not always tell them everything for "he who tells all tells little, for at the end we longer listen to him."[18] The student may not be the smartest person in the room but with the ability to learn through discovery, he will develop the love for learning. The educator's purpose "is not at all to give him knowledge, but to teach him to acquire

---

[16] E.D. Hirsh told us that in the "ever-shifting economic scene, the student needs the ability to learn new occupations. Hence, a general ability to learn, based on broad general knowledge and vocabulary, is a more practical tool than direct vocational training." Hirsch, "*The Schools We Need and Why We Don't Have Them*," p. 110.

[17] Rousseau, "*Emile (or Treatise on Education)*," p. 143.

[18] Ibid., p. 222.

it when necessary, to make him estimate it exactly for what it is worth, and to make him love truth above everything else."[19]

Benjamin Bloom wrote, "If students develop good study habits, devote more time to the learning, improve their reading skills, and so on, they will be better able to learn from a particular teacher and course—even though neither the course nor the teacher has undergone a change process."[20] Ken Robinson reminded us that a good teacher teaches the subject whereas a great teacher teaches the students.[21]

But teachers are often unaware of the fact that they are biased—who favor teaching some students and not others. They give more focus and encouragement to some students but not to others, ignoring the latter group of students although the impression they have is that their students in their classes are given quality of opportunity and attention for learning. This makes it more important for students to learn how to learn particular in large classes in higher education institutions. It is up to the students themselves to make a difference in the outcome.

In this regard, the greatest gift a teacher can give to their students is to help them discover the methods of learning and learn how to learn. It is not about studying all the time. It is about studying smart. Many books have been written on this topic. The book I find really interesting and useful is *Learning How to Learn* by Barbara Oakley, Terence Sejnowski, and Alistair McConville (OSM hereafter).[22] Below, I highlight several tools that are discussed in the book, which teachers should share with their students.

- First, students must relax their mind where they think of nothing in particular. This is especially important when students are stuck with a difficult problem. During the break, OSM advised students to do something different. When the brain is relaxed, the brain is quietly working on the problem although they would hardly notice it. There are many ways to

---

[19] Ibid., p. 189.
[20] Bloom, "*The 2 Sigma Problem*," p. 7.
[21] Robinson, "*The Element*," p. 259.
[22] Oakley and Sejnowski (with McConville), "*Learning How to Learn*."

relax such as playing a sport, listening to music, drawing, and painting.
- Second, students should avoid working last minute to study or prepare for the examinations. It will make learning harder because there is lesser time to learn. OSM wrote; "You will get stressed, miss deadlines, and not learn things properly. You get can really behind."[23] Whatever students have learned in class can be forgotten if they do not review the material, and they will have to focus and learn the same material all over again from the beginning.
- Third, it is important that students get enough sleep and exercise. Learning can take place when we sleep. During sleep, the brain recalls what we have learned during the day. The neurons continue to learn and make connections with each other, building on the neural pathway while we sleep. When we sleep, the brain transfers what we have learned (neurons in the hippocampus, home to working memory) into the cerebral cortex (home to long term memory), freeing up the brain to learn new things.[24] This is another reason why it is important for students to continuously review the material rather the cramming. Getting enough exercise is equally important. Body movement does not only work to stimulate recollection, it also enables the brain to produce chemicals such as dopamine and serotonin that can help neurons to grow. Exercise enables the brain to develop new ideas and link new ideas to old ones.[25]

---

[23] Ibid., p. 38.

[24] When we sleep, we dream. Dream has far reaching impact on learning. In "The Interpretation of Dreams," Sigmund Freud wrote that "the dream has the ability to take up the intellectual work of the day and bring to a conclusion what has not been settled during the day, that it can solve doubt and problems, and that it may become the source of new inspiration in poets and composers, seems to be indisputable." Freud, "*The Best of Sigmund Freud*," p. 66.

[25] Beethoven, Dickens, and Kierkegaard were all devotees of the long afternoon stroll.

- Fourth, OSM suggested useful ways to improve our ability to remember. They categorize information into two groups—facts and pictures. Facts are harder to remember because they are abstracts and we cannot easily picture them in our mind. Picture information on the other hand is easier to remember such as the route to take from your school to your house or the layout of the living room in your house. One way to remember the facts is to convert the facts into pictures. As OSM illustrated in their book, to remember that eating arsenic is bad, one can picture a man vomiting after eating arsenic. Other useful techniques to help us remember the information include making up metaphors like linking locker with long-term memory and a school bag with working memory, taking good handwritten notes (rather than typing them out), and teaching the information to friends and relatives.
- Fifth, practice is important to reinforce understanding. The working memory cannot handle too much information. One can get confused trying to figure out things when there is too much information. Practice helps the brain to hold on to the information. Students should not just read the notes or books. They should do something with the information such as working on a set of problems related to the topic they have learned. Students should avoid lazy learning by spending time on easy stuff and material that they already know. Teachers could get their students to try solving harder and more challenging problems. To practice, students can teach their friends. OSM advised students to do this without notes so as to strengthen understanding and to identify gaps in knowledge.
- Sixth, in an examination, OSM suggested that students pick the harder problems to work on first. If they are stuck with the harder problems, students should leave them and proceed to try the easier questions. The authors reason that by doing the harder problems first, the brain can be used as a "double processor." When students leave the harder problem incomplete and proceed to work on the easier problem, the brain focuses

on the easier problem but another part of the brain which is more relaxed and free work in the background on the harder problem. This other part of the brain is the "diffuse mode," which can make imaginative connections between ideas to generate creative solutions. If students are to wait until the end to work on the harder problem, they are preventing the diffuse mode from working to help them do better in the assignment.

- Seventh, a useful way for students to learn is to learn in groups with persons who share what they love doing. The group members can be collaborators or competitors. They may share similar vision or otherwise. What connects the members is commitment to the work that the members enjoy doing. Students help and encourage each other when they have difficulties and review the material to raise the level of learning. Finding the right members provides the inspiration and provocation to the raise the bar on students' achievements.

How Do We Know If the Educator Is Effective?

A widely used method to measure teaching effectiveness is to consider teacher's contribution to student achievement. For example, the subject passing rate is one of the indicators to infer the teacher's knowledge of the subject, his or her commitment, and teaching skills. The measure has received much attention as it seems to encourage teachers to dump down the curriculum and avoid teaching difficult concepts in order to achieve the desired and targeted passing rate.

Another common measure of teaching effectiveness is student perception of the teacher. Students evaluate the performance of the teacher, typically toward the end of the course, by completing a structured survey form. The results are tabulated to reflect the overall effectiveness of the teaching staff. Again, to secure a good rating from students, teachers may engage in improper and unprofessional practices because of the association between the survey results and reward such as promotional prospect of the teacher, tenure for university professors and more teaching assignments for sessional staff.

A useful consideration is situated in the type of activities and conduct observed in the classroom, and the ways the activities are conducted. This is contingent on the teachers' belief in the students' ability and willingness to learn to the extent that teachers who are fair and passionate about teaching is more likely to perform better than others. This approach was advocated by Bert Creemers and Leonidas Kyriakides. Table 7.1 provides a summary of good practices.

Table 7.1 A model of educational effectiveness[26]

Orientation	Providing the objectives for which a specific task/lesson/series of lessons take(s) place Challenging students to identify the reason why an activity is taking place in the lesson
Structuring	Beginning with overviews and/or review of objectives Outlining the content to be covered and signaling transitions between lesson parts Drawing attention to and reviewing main ideas
Questioning	Raising different types of questions (i.e., process and product) at appropriate difficulty level Giving time for students to respond Dealing with student responses
Teaching modelling	Encouraging students to use problem-solving strategies presented by the teacher or other classmates Inviting students to develop strategies Promoting the idea of modelling
Application	Using seatwork or small-group tasks in order to provide needed practice and application opportunities Using application tasks as starting points for the next step of teaching and learning
The classroom as a learning environment	Establishing on-task behavior through the interactions they promote (i.e., teacher-student and student–student interactions) Dealing with classroom disorder and student competition through establishing rules, persuading students to respect them and using the rules
Management of time	Organize the classroom environment Maximizing engagement rates
Assessment	Using appropriate techniques to collect data on student knowledge and skills Analyzing data in order to identify student needs and report the results to students and parents Teachers evaluating their own practices

---

[26] Creemers and Kyriakides, "*Critical Analysis of the Current Approaches to Modelling Educational Effectiveness.*"

Evidences can be gathered, using relevant metrics, to assess teaching effectiveness through class observation by a fellow academic. A popular framework that can provide some indication of the appropriate metrics to use for this purpose is derived by Charlotte Danielson, which considers four dimensions of teaching—planning and preparation, classroom observation, instruction, and professional responsibilities. The framework goes beyond mere classroom observation on content knowledge, quality of instruction, and classroom management skills to include the teacher's professional behavior such as their willingness to work with parents and stakeholders (colleagues in nonacademic functions) and participation in professional development (Table 7.2). The results can then be triangulated with student outcome and student evaluation scores to offer a credible assessment of teacher quality.

Table 7.2 Danielson's framework for teaching[27]

Planning and preparation	Demonstrating knowledge of content and pedagogy Demonstrating knowledge of students Setting instructional outcomes Demonstrating knowledge of resources Designing coherent instruction Designing student assessments
Classroom environment	Creating an environment of respect and rapport Establishing a culture for learning Managing classroom procedures Managing student behavior Organizing physical space
Instruction	Communicating with students Using questioning and discussion techniques Engaging students in learning Using assessment in instruction Demonstrating flexibility and responsiveness
Professional responsibilities	Reflecting on teaching Maintaining accurate records Communicating with families Participating in the professional community Growing and developing professionally Showing professionalism

---

[27] Danielson, *"Enhancing Professional Practice."* See also Coe, Aloisi, Higgins, and Major, *"What Makes Great Teaching?"* pp. 13–14.

All said, teaching is as much an art than a science. Effectiveness of teacher goes beyond grades and passing rates. Teachers need to include people management and relationship building as part of their duties. I am always fascinated with how some teachers who are able to capture the attention of the audience with humor, intellectual, and humility. Students show interest in class, attend the lessons regularly, and complete the required assessment tasks and eventually pass the course and graduate.

Students pursuing an education have an aspiration level. Once the aspiration is met, they will find ways to complete the course. Teachers need to believe that students can make it through their studies. The teacher can do his part by helping students set goals, and device step by step plans so that students can see incremental improvement in their effort along the way. Students have their own language, and it requires effort from the teachers to listen, think like them and try to understand them. Teachers should demonstrate their willingness to learn from students as much as they want to the students to learn from them. It helps to be humble. Tell students about your stories, your struggles and how you have learned from your mistakes. These can be inspiring.

CHAPTER 8

Leadership in Higher Education

Balancing the business and educational goals of higher education institutions (HEIs) in the private sector is one of the greatest challenges for HEI leaders.[1] As a business entity, HEIs seek for growth, market share, and profit. The key source of expansion is increase in the number of students. Where recruitment of students proves difficult, some of the HEIs may resort to lowering the entry requirements to admit more students to their courses. The academics may be pressured to ease students' progress to the next level of study to remain employed thereby raising fundamentally serious issues about the relevance of education. These measures also go against the notion of providing quality education, which serves as the other pillar of success for the HEIs.

---

[1] While this chapter makes particular reference to private education institutions, the discussion points can be relevant to public education institutions. Public education institutions are increasingly driven by market forces and commercial needs. Since the mid-1980s, federal research spending in the United States, to take an example, has stagnated while demands financial capital have risen to improve facilities and recruit star professors due to increased competition, leading higher education institutions to pursue market efficiency and alternative sources of funding through academic-industry ties and student enrolment. Commercial forces and corporate funding in universities has resulted in a number of problems, including delay in publications of research output, less sharing of academic research, manipulation of research findings to serve commercial interest and pouring of money into commercially promising courses such as computer science and biotechnology and scaling back on humanities. See Washburn, "*University, Inc.*"

How should the HEIs balance the educational and commercial goals to avoid the awkward situation where commercial interest overrides everything else? The agency theory with the executive managers as agents and the stakeholders as principals offers a theoretical framework to describe the governance issue that may lead to improper behavior. External and internal measures can be applied to curb excessive focus on the commercial aspect of the business. External measures include listing rules imposed on public listed companies and the appointment of external auditors to highlight issues in the governance and reporting of the companies. Internal measures include appointment of nonexecutive directors and separating the role of the Board Chairman and Chief Executive Officer.

This chapter discusses the inadequacy of the internal and external controls in the context of higher education and argues that ethical decision must be derived from within the organization and championed by the leaders. Leaders in the education field refer to the management team, consisting of the Chief Executive Officers, Academic Deans, and Department Heads. A key message of this chapter centers on the importance of responsible leadership in building and sustaining a business and incorporating the interest of multiple stakeholders.

Improper Practices in Higher Education

Worldwide, HEIs in the private sector account for a third of the total student enrolment and a greater percentage of total HEIs.[2] Citing data from Pathenon-EY, *The Economist* has reported that the number of students enrolled in private higher education has grown at a faster rate than those in the public sector in Turkey, France, Germany, and Spain.[3] In Chile, the number of private universities has increased from 6 in 1980 to 45 in 2010, accounting for 78 percent of the total number of universities and enrolling 70 percent of the total student population.[4] In Mexico, the

---

[2] See Levy, "*The Unanticipated Explosion*"; Gupta, "*International Trends and Private Higher Education in India.*"
[3] See McDermott, "*Class Apart.*"
[4] Gregorutti, Espinoza, Gonzales and Loyola, "*What if Privatizing Higher Education Becomes an Issue?*"

number of private universities has grown from 148 in 1980 to 1,740 in 2010, which represents 67 percent of the total number of universities in the country. About one-third of the total student population is enrolled in the private universities. James Tooley points out that private education is a burgeoning sector in a great majority of countries.[5] In Indonesia, 23 percent of primary and secondary school students are in the private sector. The sector accounts for 94 percent of higher education students. The need to restrain public expenditure on education to reduce budget deficits and external debts has led to the surge of the private education providers to fill the gap and absorb the demand for higher education.[6]

However, the profit motive of the education providers has been associated with issues of low-quality academic standards.[7] Profit-making education providers have been accused of allowing students to ignore strict academic standards in terms of assessment and attendance.[8] The education providers have also been recruiting academic staff with marginal qualifications to save costs and of pegging the curricula to the minimal standards.[9] Opponents have pointed to the lack of academic integrity, for example, by maximizing class size thereby creating a nonconducive environment for learning. This concern has been exacerbated by the lack of transparency in both academic and nonacademic aspects.[10]

In Chile and Mexico, the expansion of private education sector has not led to improved quality. On the contrary, qualifications attained from

---

[5] Tooley, "*The Global Education Industry.*"

[6] Longden and Belanger, "*Universities*"; Enders, De Boer and Weyer, "*Regulatory Autonomy and Performance.*"

[7] See Harman, "*Australian Academics and Prospective Academics*"; Marks, "*The Unsettled Meaning of Undergraduate Education in a Competitive Higher Education Environment*"; Ward, "*Academic Values, Institutional Management and Public Policies.*"

[8] Bryman, "*Effective Leadership in Higher Education*"; Lechuga, "*Assessment, Knowledge, And Customer Service.*"

[9] Bernasconi, "*The Profit Motive in Higher Education.*"

[10] For details, see Pitcher, "*Managing the Tensions Between Maintaining Academic Standards and the Commercial Imperative in a UK Private Sector Higher Education Institution*"; Lok, Gazi Mahabubul Alam, and Abdul Rahman Idris, "*Balancing Managerial and Academic Values.*"

the HEIs have been mired with low-quality problems due to a lack of effective systems of accreditation.[11] In February 2008, two private schools in Singapore, Camford Business School and Boston International, were reported to have employed dubious practice by offering degrees from unaccredited universities. Camford Business School offered degrees from Paramount University of Technology, a well-known degree mill institution based in Wyoming in the United States whereas Boston International was alleged to have worked with a "West Coast University," which has received accreditation by an agency in the South Pacific Islands of Wallis and Futuna.[12]

In the United States, the federal government won a major court case against Corinthian College Inc in the late 2015. The latter was alleged to have advertised false placement rates by hiring its own graduates to recruit students and swindled students to take out private loans at a higher interest rate. The now defunct for-profit school, which oversaw 100 schools in states such as California, Oregon, and Arizona, was asked to pay back U.S. $531 million in damages to students in October 2015.[13]

When commercial goals constitute an important part of the business, there is a danger that the commercial goals may override other interests. The for-profit HEIs are especially vulnerable because the management team consists of pro-salespersons, including the Head of Sales Unit and Head of the Marketing and Branding Unit. While the composition of key leaders in the HEIs is reflective of the private education landscape, it also signals the commercial orientation of the HEIs, and the possibility that decisions are made strictly on business sense with less perspectives from the academic side.[14]

---

[11] As discussed in Gregorutti, Espinoza, Gonzales and Loyola, "*What if Privatizing Higher Education Becomes an Issue?*"

[12] As discussed in Sam, "*Private Education in Singapore.*"

[13] The US Department of Education has earlier fined the college US$30 million for overstating the job placement rates. See Nasiripour, "*Obama to Cancel Debts Owned by Defrauded For-Profit College Students*"; Green, "*Will Corinthian Colleges Be Able to Pay Back Students?*"

[14] There have been concerns that Academic Deans of for-profit education providers are pressured to meet financial targets at the expense of maintaining academic quality. See De Boer and Goedegebuure, "*The Changing Nature of the Academic Deanship*"; Montez, Wolverton, and Gmelch, "*The Roles and Challenges of Deans.*"

University administrators and the academics are sometimes at loggerheads. University administrators are frustrated with the educators for pointing fingers and pointing the blame on students for weak performance. And that students who receive the higher education qualifications are often unprepared for the modern workplace. They also feel that educators focus almost exclusively on academic subjects and are resistant to help learners engage in critical thinking, problem-solving, and taking responsibility.

At the same time, educators are frustrated with the administrators for meddling in their affairs. They dislike the fact that HEIs accept almost any applicants who walk in the door at any time. It does not matter that the candidates lack the language proficiency or does not want to join the course nor the school. Educators are unhappy that the HEIs do not entertain the idea of laying off the lowest performing students who have no whatsoever means to meet the graduation requirements. Because their employment with the HEIs is dependent on the teaching performance, there is the potential risk of some faculty members lowering the academic standards so as to accommodate the capabilities of students who struggled to pass the subjects and complete the course, or they do so in order for them to receive positive student evaluations and maintain employment.

Agency Theory and Its Limitations

The agency theory offers a theoretical framework to describe the relationship between the stakeholders and professional managers. The shareholders are owners of the business, but they do not control the use of resources nor make day-to-day decisions. These tasks are carried out by the professional managers, the agents. The agency theory argues that the agents should serve the interests of the shareholders, the principals.

Concerns arise when the agents make decisions that maximize their personal interest or tarnish the reputation of the firm with the shareholders facing problems in monitoring the agents. There are various ways in which the agency problem can surface in the private education sector. Professional managers in HEIs may expropriate company funds to travel excessively and furnish their offices with unnecessary gadgets instead of returning any excess cash to the shareholders. They may artificially overstate revenue and gains and hide expenses to inflate the bottom line.

In procurement (of teaching materials, stationary, laboratory equipment, and others), it may be possible for a manager to purchase materials at a higher price because he or she has received bribes from the vendor.

To mitigate the problem, two forms of control mechanisms may be introduced. First, the external framework can be put in place to manage reputational risk and demand that the firm serves the interests of stakeholders. Specific legal protection can be enacted to protect the students (e.g., the protection of students' fees in the event the HEI is unable to continue operation due to insolvency and/or regulatory closure), the employees (the right to unionize and bargain in good faith), and local communities (constrain management from damaging the reputation of the country). Regulations have existed in industries to constraint the market for corporate control. Mergers in the banking industry, for instance, must obtain regulatory approval.

Indeed, regulatory measures in the private education sector have been introduced to protect students' interest and regulate the behavior of the HEIs. In Singapore, the Council for Private Education (CPE) of Singapore (established in 2009) serves as the external control agency, looking over matters such as registration, quality assurance, investigation, and enforcement action against errant commercial HEIs. The interest of students is especially important for the CPE. For example, all EduTrust-certified private education providers must subscribe to the Fee Protection Scheme (FPS) with CPE-approved insurance service providers before they are allowed to collect more than two months of course fees at any one time.[15]

In Malaysia, the National Accreditation Board Act of 1996 provided for the establishment of the National Accreditation Board (NAB) to formulate policies on standards and quality of the programs, and grant official approval and accreditation to certificates, diplomas, and degrees awarded by the HEIs. In 2005, the government adopted the Malaysian

---

[15] CPE was renamed Committee for Private Education in October 2016. EduTrust certification is mandatory for HEIs in Singapore to admit international students. Limiting the amount of fees collected upfront and the insurance provision is deemed necessary to minimize the financial impact of sudden closure of the HEIs on the students in the event that the HEIs fail or refuse to be a member of the fee protection scheme.

Quality Framework to assess the HEI courses and programs, which has been used by the Quality Assurance Division (QAD) to assess public education providers that follow the national education system. Two years later, the Malaysian cabinet approved the merger of NAB and QAD to form the Malaysian Qualifications Agency as the sole accreditation agency for both public and private HEIs.[16] In the case of Argentina, the regulatory agency imposes strict rules on the HEIs, including time schedules for classes, the use of only approved textbooks by the Ministry of Education and staff movement.[17]

But no amount of external control can eradicate improper practices. The corporate scandals in the 2000s that affected some large private sector corporations such as Enron, WorldCom in the United States, and Parmalat and Royal Ahold in Europe are illustrative.[18] The corporate scandals revealed not only failings of corporate governance or of business regulations but also more importantly the problems of corporate leadership. Leaders such as William Ebber (WorldCom), Kenneth Lay (Enron), and Dennis Kozlowski (Tyco) were obsessed with retaining power, deceiving the investors and markets with inflated financial statements—a result of a complex web of special purpose mechanisms that managed to keep losses out of the company's net profit calculation and to keep debt off its balance sheet.

Another concern with regulatory control is that it may only appear in form rather than in substance in dealing with unethical practices. In Chile, while the government has established the National Commission for Accreditation of Undergraduate Program (NAP) in 1999 to design and implement a national system of quality assurance of all HEIs, conflict of interest arises when the accreditation agencies approved by the National Accreditation Commission have consulting committees engaged by the HEIs seeking to get accreditation, prompting the Chilean government to

---

[16] See Tan, "*Malaysian Private Higher Education*"; Tham, "*Internationalizing Higher Education in Malaysia.*"

[17] See Tooley, "*The Global Education Industry.*"

[18] Enron was monitored by no less than eight gatekeepers and monitors. Yet, few if any were able to identify any wrongdoings.

hire an international body to review the entire system of accreditation in the country.[19]

In addition, there are certain aspects of governance that are not covered by the regulatory agency. In Singapore, the CPE has focused almost exclusively on the development and implementation of procedure and processes. But the current regulatory system is not able to accurately reflect quality differences among the HEIs and therefore offers minimal additional benefits to the HEIs that have emphasized academic excellence more than others. It is possible that rules are enacted and accepted because they are considered as the right rules by the regulatory agency but they do not necessarily mean that the results or outcomes are in themselves good.

Internal controls are primarily associated with the set of rules and procedures (such as incentive schemes) to align the interests of the agents to that of the principals. For example, remunerating Program Consultants or Sales Executives through commission is a common practice in the HEIs so that they are rewarded (more extensively) only upon successful recruitment of students into courses and programs. But internal control mechanisms cannot possibly make leaders display responsible behaviors that would benefit the stakeholders nor is it possible for external controls to alter the outcome of leaders' decisions if the leaders are unable or unclear of what constitute as a responsible leader. The requisite for effective internal control devices rests on the type of leaders who are heading the HEIs. What is crucial is that leaders must be prepared to leave the assumptions of the profit maximization world and work toward maximization of students' interest. The motivation to lead responsibly must come from the leaders themselves.

In summary, both internal and external controls are mired with problems. Balancing commercial and educational objectives in the HEIs requires the presence of true leaders—responsible leaders who are committed to do the right thing and ensure that the followers display the same commitment. But what would constitute as essential elements of a responsible leader in the education sector?

---

[19] See Gregorutti, Espinoza, Gonzales and Loyola, "*What if Privatizing Higher Education Becomes an Issue?*"

Why Is Leadership Important?

Leaders play an important role in an organization. Change will not happen without leadership. Leaders have to step forward and get involved with change for it to take place.[20]

Effective leadership goes beyond educational qualifications. It touches aspects of character. Unlike intellectual competence, which can be measured, for example, using IQ test, it is much more difficult to measure character. But character matters in dealing with dilemmas and is often touted as one of the most important personal characteristics of the leader—someone who is seen as trusted, who has high integrity, and who is truthful and honest.[21]

Earlier, I have alluded to the challenges faced by HEI leaders—to reconcile the business and educational objectives. As a business entity, the leaders are responsible to the business owners and therefore required their attention to grow and expand the business. As an education provider, the leaders are responsible in ensuring that students gain from acquiring a qualification that would enable them to effectively participate in the business community.

It is important for the HEI leaders to understand what it takes to be responsible leaders. Given the power of the HEI leaders and the role of education in general as enabler of personal and societal growth and development, HEI leaders have to take a more active role and acknowledge their responsibility to care for the needs of the multiple stakeholders.

To be sure, a responsible leader does not have to be one who must possess "higher moral standard" than the rest as Joanne Ciulla has convincingly argued. Nor is it necessary for the HEI to abandon its profit motive. No for-profit education provider can survive without profit.[22] What we need are leaders who understand the need and have the

---

[20] Without leaders, initiatives do not get started in the first place. As Max De Pree told us, leaders can delegate efficiency to someone else but they must deal personally with effectiveness. De Pree, "*Leadership Is an Art.*"

[21] See, for example, Kouzes and Poster, "*Credibility.*"

[22] Ciulla, "*Carving Leaders From the Warped Wood of Humanity.*"

capability to strike a right balance the power between commercial interest and student interest.

We need leaders with wisdom and self-control—leaders who give more thought for the long-term future of higher education. Long-term thinking is often difficult. Short-term thinking normally prevails. Because it is not too distant from the far future, leaders feel more anxious and excited about the short term. They can imagine events that can take place soon such as rewards for jobs well done. However, short-term thinking and long-term thinking are not unconnected. The future is often the cumulative actions and reactions to what is happening in the present. Because the future is created step-by-step, we naturally feel that the future to be like the present albeit, deviating from the starting point. The connection between short-term goals and long-term aspirations are essential to allow us to take corrective actions when targets are not met and avoid a situation where we feel exhausted. Leaders must avoid thinking about the short term without regard to what they feel the future is when they get there (e.g., we focus on the how, driven by the KPIs, and pay lesser or no attention to the why).

In dealing with ethical dilemma there is no such thing as ready solution made in advance. We can refer to past experiences, case studies, theoretical underpinnings and consider the best practical experience that fit the collective needs and demands. We judge an idea to be acceptable because we are able to frame the idea to a favorable situation that is more valuable than other options. Whether we treat students as customers or as students, colleges and universities must provide the necessary means fitted to facilitate the transformation of the students through the education process. The conditions must always be perfectly designed to ensure it.

Responsible Leadership

Thomas Maak and Nicola Pless define responsible leadership as "a relational and ethical phenomenon, which occurs in social processes of interaction and have a stake in the purpose and vision of the leadership relationships."[23] To Maak and Pless, a responsible leader is one

---

[23] Maak and Pless, "*Responsible Leadership in a Stakeholder Society,*" p. 103.

who possesses high relationship intelligence, a product of the ethical dimension (make decisions that are drawn on moral norms) and emotional intelligence, which highlights the importance of understanding and managing emotions to enhance personal growth and social relations and using emotions to facilitate thought. Responsible leadership in this regard should consist of bravado in constructing a student-centric learning and teaching environment, doing the right thing and accepting short-term consequences even if they may be harmful to the education provider from the commercial standpoint.

Susan Lynham and Thomas Chermack device a theoretical model known as the Responsible Leadership for Performance (RLP), which emphasizes the whole system effect—the consideration of the constituency in setting the objectives that forms the first input in the model, the importance of a leader to demonstrate effectiveness, ethical decision making, and endurance in the course of his or her work and the ability of the leader to focus on performance.[24] By performance, they were referring "to the activity and the outcome of the activity" and not the latter alone.[25] The domain of performance may include the mission and purpose of the organization, work processes and individual performance. The specific role of a responsible leader in this regard does not resonate with the traditional role of leaders that focuses on how the followers are influenced to achieve a certain result. Instead, the organizational leaders are expected to build good relationship with the staff to advance the organization's cause.

A responsible leader is expected to consider the stakeholders' interest as opposed to merely the interest of the shareholders or business owners, recognize net wealth maximization as the objective of private corporations, and that each stakeholder, including the consumers, suppliers, and employees, has the right to be treated as means to some end.

What are the roles of a responsible leader in higher education?

First and foremost, a responsible leader pays attention to the interest of the stakeholders. Archie Carroll has identified four components of corporate social responsibility—economic, legal, discretionary/

---

[24] Lynham and Chermack, "*Responsible Leadership for Performance.*"
[25] Dean, "*Dale Breathier*," p. 72.

philanthropic, and ethical—which offers a useful framework for analysis (Table 8.1).[26]

Table 8.1 Corporate social responsibility components in higher education institutions[27]

Component of CSR	Social expectation	HEI behavior and decisions	Normative prescription
Economic responsibility	Required of business by society	Maximize student population Minimize cost	Be profitable
Legal responsibility	Required of business by society	Comply with laws and regulations	Obey the law
Ethical responsibility	Expected of business by society	Emphasis academic quality Student centricity	Be ethical
Discretionary/ Philanthropic responsibility	Desired of business by society	Engage in community programs	Be a good corporate citizen

Economic responsibility places the business as an economic institution in which profit making represents an essential responsibility of the free enterprise. HEIs are expected to make strategic decisions to maximize student population and minimize costs. Legal responsibility is about obeying the law and code of conduct. HEIs are expected to comply with regulations, stipulating the requirements to establish the academic board, insure school fees to protect student interest against bankruptcy, and communicate policy changes to students, among others. The laws establish the ground rules under which the HEIs are expected to comply to remain in business.

Discretionary or philanthropic responsibility is concerned with business involvement in social events and activities that are not mandated by law or expected of the business by the society. For education providers, philanthropic responsibility includes creating meaningful platforms for students to do their part for society by working with the local communities through food donation and fund-raising activities. Consider the

---

[26] Carroll, *"Stakeholder Thinking in Three Models of Management."*
[27] Ibid., p. 50.

following examples of HEIs that have actively engaged in social responsibility programs.

- Objectivo/UNIP, a chain of private schools and universities in Brazil, offers free services for the community through the dentistry and law departments.
- New International School of Thailand, a private school founded in 1992, offers programs for its students to get involved in community services; for example, teaching English to disadvantaged students in Bangkok and in the countryside.

Ethical responsibility represents practices or behaviors that are not codified into laws, but it is expected of the education institutions to reflect its concern about students, employees, and the community. Some of the institutes of higher learning see higher education as a moral education to get students identify with something that is bigger than the self. For example, higher education across the Jesuit network is committed to the development of the whole person, integrating intellectual, religion, and social dimensions into the curricula. Higher education in the Jesuit tradition seeks to build a more peaceful and just world by exposing students to local, regional, and global experiences and interdisciplinary study of issues such as migration, poverty, inequality, human rights, and climate change.

For profit-making organizations, as Carroll pointed out, an ethical leader strives to make profit but the "pursuit of profit is done within the confines of sound legal and ethical precepts such as justice, due process and the protection of stakeholders' rights." Ethical leaders "comply both with the letter and the spirits of law," which are seen as the floor on ethical behavior. "Moral managers strive to operate well above and beyond what law mandates."[28] Examples of moral management in the higher education sector include:

- Provision of language support program to students to help them cope with their academic courses.
- Provision of a transition program for progressing students.

---

[28] Ibid., p. 53.

- Direct students to an alternative education provider that offers a course that matches the student's wants and capabilities.
- Fair treatment for teaching staff by providing them with time and resources to engage students constructively.

Second, to undertake the ethical role, a responsible leader has to emphasize growth through *relationship* building. A responsible leader in the HEIs places the organization as part of the larger community. They see sustaining employee morale, establishing long-term relationship with partner universities, community members, and business leaders, and having a good relationship with the government as essential obligations and foundations of their success.

A responsible leader in the HEI strives to balance the commercial and educational demands, giving neither more emphasis than the other, and demonstrate his or her capability to lead with integrity. This requires a leader who is able to assume the *stewardship* position to safeguard personal and professional values and resources. As a steward, Maak and Pless wrote, a responsible leader navigates in a world of "complexity, uncertainty, change, and conflict interests" and "protect personal and professional integrity, and steering a business responsibly and respectfully, even though troubled (global) waters, thus protecting and preserving what one is entrusted with."[29]

The establishment of the vision statement and core values is an important exercise in this regard to help staff and agents ascertain what is right and what is wrong. The leaders' role is to translate the values into actions, using the values to define the boundaries and act as reference points when the organization is under pressure. Hence, if the vision of the HEI to be a quality education provider, the leader ensures that quality is protected and that he/she is able to withstand the pressure to increase student population through improper means like significantly lowering the entry requirements. An organization that values the stakeholders' interest builds on ethically sound vision and core values, and it is the duty of the leader to ensure that these are followed through.

---

[29] Maak and Pless, *"Responsible Leadership In A Stakeholder Society,"* p. 108.

The values and assumptions shared by responsible leaders help to legitimize ways of thinking by ruling-in certain ways of talking about issues and ruling-out other approaches. Newly recruited employees should be taught and educated about the organizational values and assumptions. Rather than letting them gain more in-depth understanding of the business over time, deliberate effort should be put in to align the employees' thought process with the business. As leaders, they are the role models for others for the type of behavior they want to encourage. If they are not effective leaders or role models from the start, others will not believe what they say. A responsible leader therefore has the duty to inculcate the values to the followers and be someone others could trust to deal with conflicting interest. The responsibility leader must possess good communication skills and architectural skills to "create and cultivate a work environment where diverse individuals find meaning, feel respected, recognised and included ... to contribute to their highest potential, both in a business and a moral sense."[30]

Third, a responsible leader serves the interest of the others and cares for their needs.[31] Serving others in the education setting means ensuring a safe and healthy place for work and study, promoting a holistic education that allows students to identify and develop their strengths, providing an education qualification that is valued by the employers, and producing graduates who can contribute effectiveness in the business community regardless of gender, nationality, race, and religion. A servant leader is more inclined to contribute to the success of students than making money for the shareholders. To help students who are unable to pay their school fees, leaders in Koc University, a private university from Turkey, offers students part-time employment opportunities so that they can complete their education.

Responsible leaders, as servant leaders, take time to develop purposes—the objectives they want to achieve. They have plans to see how the purposes can be achieved, spread them out over a period of time so that the educators and administrators do not feel overwhelmed and

---

[30] Ibid., p. 111.
[31] See Greenleaf, *"Servant Leadership."*

that there is enough time to do proper preparation and planning. Responsible leaders establish teams, recognize and reward successes, communicate plans, engage students, and avoid check-up of the staff too much and too often (i.e., avoid micromanaging) to achieve organizational change successfully.

Fourth, a responsible leader in the higher education sector must be *effective* in delivery. At the end of the day, leaders are judged by their ability to achieve the planned goals and objectives. Certainly, financial goals are set and the HEI is expected to achieve them. But the HEI should not focus merely on the outcomes but also on how the decisions are arrived. A way forward is to consider academic excellence and reputation as reference points in planning and decision making. Attainment of a good reputation sustains organizations' competitive advantage and makes them more attractive to the consumers.[32] Academic excellence and school reputation are similarly critical. Schools with a good reputation enjoy strong financial performance and positive word of mouth behaviors.[33]

For an education institution, academic excellence and reputational standard inevitably translate to strong commitment toward academic integrity and positive student learning experience.

Academic integrity—Surely, giving away answers to students in an examination does not make academic sense. Passing the student without appropriately assessing the students' ability through assessment tasks undermines the academic standard of the institution. Reputation provides the HEI with the most importance source of competitive advantage.

Academic policies relating to examinations, appeals against academic results, and plagiarism cases must be clearly stated and strictly enforced. Responsible leaders recognize that these decisions are academic in nature and ensure that the decisions rest with the academics. Minimum entry requirement for a course is another issue that requires academic judgment

---

[32] Fombrun, *"Reputation."*
[33] Safon, *"Measuring the Reputation of Top US Business Schools."*; Skallerud, *"School Reputation and its Relation to Parents' Satisfaction and Loyalty."*; Vidaver-Cohen, *"Reputation Beyond the Rankings."*

unclouded by commercial goals. Lowering the entry requirements allows the HEIs to admit more students therefore representing an attractive proposition for the HEI to meet its revenue objective. If the entry requirements are set too low, students face difficulty coping with the demands of the program. When students fail in the subjects and begin to drop out from their studies, the pressure is on the academics to keep them in the system, which often involves lowering the academic rigor and standard. To the irresponsible leaders, enrolment and retention rates are what matter. Being a responsible and effective leader in this regard is about the leader's willingness and ability to demarcate the business and academic units; for example, by preventing the academics from taking full responsibility for making decisions that are tied to financial goals.

All functions in the HEIs must have clear roles and responsibilities. When commercial and educational objectives clash, certain emotional issues with arise. To deal with the issues effectively, leaders must be able to listen with an open mind and understand the different and contrasting viewpoints coming from various sources and to assess the implications on the organization. Only when they truly understand what is happening can they offer a way to resolve the conflict. An organization consists of a dynamic system, each function creating effects everywhere, holding the organization together.

To deal with dilemmas and conflicts, a leader should not view leadership as merely they standing on top of the mountain, thinking strategically and inspire people with visions. A responsible leader has to engage the people thoroughly and comprehensively and understand the business and the industry. A responsible leader uses his knowledge of the business to probe and question to encourage the employees to think about the issues. A responsible leader is intensely involved with the operations, know the realities on the ground and knowledgeable about the details to arrive at a decision. The leader asks tough questions that everyone else must answer, debate the information and strike the right trade-offs. It is about encouraging debate, dialogue, open discussion, and reaching an agreement to that follow through plans can be executed.

A responsible leader will try to balance the inconsistences by building certain assumptions around the issues that overtime become part of the organizational culture.[34] For instance, creating the culture can entail instilling the mindset of strong student learning support system, to track students' progress and identify and assist weaker students. The staff who recruit students into the courses have to work with the academic staff to review the admission requirements. Students who are admitted into the courses via the nonstandard route must be supported with measures to help them cope with their studies even if this increases the operating expenses. A responsible leader in this regard must be able to identify diversity in functions, handle them sensitively and with respect. It is about forging relationship—with people, information, events, and ideas, and participating in the relationship to contribute to the whole. Leaders could not simply order change or imagine that conflicts will resolve by themselves or that transitions are automatic.

Student centricity—The importance attached to customers is succinctly summarized by Sam Walton, founder of Walmart, in the following words: "There is one boss—the customer. And he can fire everybody in the company from the chairman on down, simply by spending his money somewhere else."[35] This applies to the higher education sector. Students who have a positive learning experience and receive better value are crucial sales and marketing agents for the HEIs so their actions and discussion about the HEIs in a positive way help to drive business performance forward in terms of revenue, profit, and profitability. Student centricity is not about treating customers as bosses. It is about laying the foundation of trust that will strengthen the organization's commitment to providing quality education through, for example, commitment to quality teaching.

There is a misconception that being student-centric correlates with the use of technology in teaching and learning. Identify students who need academic help early in the course (e.g., using formative assessments) and provide academic support to help them cope with their studies are some examples of a learner-centered activity that do not require significant investment in technology. Similarly, smaller classes or smaller schools with fewer students offers lecturers a fantastic opportunity to know the students better, address their concerns, and accord greater ownership to

---

[34] On organisational culture, see Schein, *"Organisational Culture and Leadership."*
[35] Quoted from Entrepreneur, *"Sam Walton."*

the students through, for example, flip teaching and presentation opportunities. Students enjoy their lessons and learn more, benefiting from smaller class size, and sharing their experience with friends and relatives. On that note, a fully online-based course does not automatically translate to more student centricity as compared to delivering the classes in person.

Student centricity is also about ensuring that all branches and franchises are subject to identical processes and procedures. Consider the case of the Education Investment Corporation Limited (Educor), the largest private education group in Southern Africa. Educor has put in place quality control procedures to ensure that the various schools under their care and control run the same courses. It also ensures that the teachers are provided with standardized course materials and the students are assessed by centrally approved assignments. All lecturers are evaluated using the standardized lecturer evaluation form.

A responsible teaching institution is learner centered. Students are supported by learning materials and resources so that they are able to complete the assessment tasks and meet the learning outcomes. Students are not misled by promotional activities into signing up for the course. There is clarity in terms of what they are signing up for, the requirements of the program, and the prospects of graduates.

The education institution appoints qualified teaching staff and provides adequate support to teachers for adoption of student-centric teaching pedagogy. Lecturers who teach a class with international students who are non-native English speakers are reminded and encouraged to adopt a different teaching approach as compared to teaching a class consisting largely of native English speakers. A responsible leader focuses on teaching quality, encouraging teachers to ease international students' transition to the academic system, for example, by writing key terms on the board to help students who are lacking in vocabulary. Good practice for education providers, as quite appropriately defined by the UNESCO and OECD, has to be "responsible for the quality as well as the social, cultural and linguistic relevance of education and the standards of qualifications provided in their name, no matter where or how it is delivered."[36]

---

[36] UNESCO and OECD, *"Guidelines for Quality Provision in Cross-Border Higher Education,"* p. 14.

While there are certain behaviors that are outright right or wrong, increasingly more people are prepared to criticize behavior which is considered as improper even it if is legal. Paying excessive bonuses to the CEOs of companies that failed to deliver a good performance is an example. The world of education is similarly clouded with gray areas. Educational leaders today are faced with ethical dilemmas and the challenge is to consider the most appropriate decision to make. The staff members have a wide range of loyalties and professional commitment, dealing with students who are themselves diverse, ranging from academically committed students to those who care less about their academic endeavors. The challenge is especially prevalent in for-profit education provides because of their necessity to consider the commercial aspect of the business. Clearly, mere compliance with the rules and regulations as stipulated by regulatory agencies nationally, regionally, and internationally is not adequate.

Although this chapter has not considered all aspects of responsible leadership, it has put forward several recommendations for leaders to consider, as summarized below:

- Responsible leaders in HEIs emphasize growth through relationship building.
- Responsible leaders in HEIs protect and maintain the reputation of the organization.
- The HEIs separates the academic and nonacademic decisions to avoid the awkward situation where commercial interest overrides every other consideration.
- Responsible leaders in HEIs develop core values and vision that resonate with followers.
- Responsible leaders in HEIs put the interest of students in everything they do.
- Responsible leaders in HEIs build an organization wide culture of academic integrity.

Epilogue

When this book goes for print, the coronavirus pandemic has taken a social, economic, and emotional toll on every country in the world. More than 250 million persons have been infected.[1] The total number of COVID-19 deaths worldwide has surpassed 5 million.[2] We are nowhere near the end of the pandemic.

The pandemic has forced higher education institutions to move to remote and online learning. Schools have arranged for teachers to visit students who do not have access to electricity or the Internet to provide in-person lessons or prepare printed instructional materials to students to pick up at convenient locations. Many have worked closely with the government and technology companies to keep teaching and learning going.[3]

The shift caused by the pandemic has prompted higher education institutions to rethink the teaching and learning model and reconsider

---

[1] The first case was reported in Wuhan City in December 2019. The impact of the coronavirus shows that the world is deeply interconnected. People are more mobile that before, travelling for work, leisure, and other purposes. As reported by Fareed Zakaria, it took less than three months for the virus to spread from Wuhan city in China where the virus was thought to first emerge to La Rioja in Argentina, which lies on the exact opposite side of the planet from Wuhan, some 12,000 miles away. Zakaria, "*Ten Lessons for a Post-Pandemic World*," p. 168.

[2] David Cutler and Lawrence Summers estimated the cumulative financial costs of the COVID-19 pandemic related to the lost output and health reduction, amounting to more than US$16 trillion, or approximately 90 percent of the United States annual Gross Domestic Product. The costs, they noted, "exceeded those associated with conventional recessions and the Iraq War, and are similar to those associated with global climate change." Cutler and Summers, "*The COVID-19 Pandemic and the $16 Trillion Virus.*"

[3] While some parents and observers rejected reopening of schools in the middle of the pandemic, others have welcomed the resumption of schools due to lack of resources at home to look after their children or high-speed Internet to allow for remote learning.

university education more broadly. One question to ask is: why do higher education institutions (HEIs) exist?

Historically, schools were located mainly in monasteries. They trained the clerics whose skills were important to the illiterate warrior tribes to rule the occupied territories. The clergy maintained law and order in the territories by recording the rules; writing contracts and decrees; and passing historical, medical, and scientific knowledge. Scholars travelled in great distances to acquire knowledge. India's Nalanda, for example, attracted intellectual scholars from China to study Buddhism and translate Sanskrit documents into Chinese in the first millennium.[4]

The Industrial Revolution of the 18th and 19th century defined the education we know today, bringing standardization of teaching methods and equipping workers with enough education to work in factories and offices. The most essential part of education, to learn to read, write, and account, is acquired to allow persons to function in the workplace.

If jobs require just a few simple steps and routine operations, then the push for acquisition of higher order skills and knowledge is not necessary. But such work is increasingly performed by machines or outsourced to others who can do them at a much lower rate. When machines replace manual work, more people are spending their working days with information and ideas. The share of jobs that involve pushing, lifting, and working with things—farm workers, operators, back-office clerical work—has fallen while those who work with information and perform problem-solving and problem-identifying work—sales, designers, consultants, managerial and professional jobs—has increased.

Students look upon the learning institutions as some places with magical power to provide them with the golden passport to good job and good life. Indeed, many have suggested that the idea of higher education is to prepare graduates for jobs that have not been created, use technologies that have not been invented, and deal with social problems that have not

---

[4] Nalanda, a Buddhist University, attracted scholars from China and elsewhere, came to an end after hundreds of years of existence at the time when universities of Oxford and Cambridge were founded in the 18th century. Some of the Chinese scholars who visited Nalanda were Yi Jing, Faxian, and Xuanzang. See Sen, "*The Argumentative Indian,*" pp. 161–174.

occurred. Critically, companies are hiring educated workers to perform the intellectual component of the work, shifting brainpower from managers to nonmanagers. Correspondingly, wage differences between graduate and nongraduate rose. In fact, a greater part of one's time is devoted to learning to engage in occupations that exert a considerable degree of knowledge and ingenuity to deal with unprogrammed challenges that are continually occurring at the workplace; otherwise rendering the person less employable and incapable of contributing to varied occupations. Students' susceptibility to overestimating the role of schools and underestimating the importance of self-effort, self-determination, and situations has implications for everything from school selection to major selection.

College life has accordingly become more competitive than before. Being in the college is no longer enough to distinguish oneself from the rest. Learning is stressful to enter reputable colleges and universities, to get good grades, and to get well-paying job thereafter as employers continue to use educational qualifications to gauge suitability of candidates. The society has imposed upon itself the necessity for persons to acquire educational qualifications, by obliging them to sit for examinations or secure professional qualifications before they can be allowed to gain employment in any corporation. It is not surprising that psychologists have noticed many teens who are depressed, anxious, and angry.

As we enter into the post-COVID world, what kind of education will be relevant to the students? When Noam Chomsky, retired professor at the Massachusetts Institute of Technology, was asked "What does it mean to be truly educated in modern times?," he answered the question this way. It is worth quoting Chomsky's response at length.

> I think I can do no better about answering the question of what it means to be truly educated than to go back to some of the classic views on the subject. For example, the views expressed by the founder of the modern higher education system, Wilhelm von Humboldt, leading humanist, a figure of the enlightenment who wrote extensively on education and human development and argued, I think, kind of very plausibly, that the core principle and requirement of a fulfilled human being is the ability to inquire and create constructively independently without external controls.

> To move to a modern counterpart, a leading physicist who talked right here [at MIT], used to tell in his classes that it is not important what we cover in the class, but it is important what you discover.
>
> To be truly educated from this point of view means to be in a position to inquire and to create on the basis of the resources available to you which you have come to appreciate and comprehend.
>
> To know where to look, to know how to formulate serious questions, to question a standard doctrine if that is appropriate, to find your own way, to shape the questions that are worth pursuing, and to develop the path to pursue them.
>
> That means knowing, understanding many things but also, much more important than what you have stored in your mind, to know where to look, how to look, how to question, how to challenge, how to proceed independently to deal with the challenges that the world presents to you and that you develop in the course of your self-education and inquiry and investigations, in cooperation and solidarity with others.
>
> That is what an educational system should cultivate from kindergarten to graduate school, and in the best cases sometimes does, and that leads to people who are, at least by my standards, well educated.[5]

If Chomsky is right, getting good grades or being smart should not be the dominant goal in education. The true value of education in the society is to enable a person to think and write clearly and appreciate knowledge for the sake of understanding the universe, the society, and ourselves. It is about educating students to be critical learners and lifelong learners.

However, hiring companies think otherwise, using academic qualifications and achievements as the signals to decide who to hire. Education qualifications have become markers of excellence, forming trust on others to perform tasks from cooking to construction and prescription of

---

[5] See the interview with Noam Chomsky: https://youtube.com/watch?v=eYHQcXVp4F4

medication. They forced us to think with the aid of categories.[6] It does not help that politicians offer themselves as smart to justify their actions and remain in office. Donald Trump has often insisted that he is "a smart person," "a very stable genius," pointing to his uncle who had been a professor at MIT to make the claim that he had "good genes, very good genes." In February 2019, Michael Cohen, Trump's former person attorney testified before Congress that Trump had threatened to sue colleges that he had attended if they were to make public his college grades and SAT scores. As Michael Sandel noted that "credentialism had become so pervasive a basis of judgment that it served as a kind of all-purpose rhetoric of credibility; deployed in moral and political combat far beyond the campus gates. The weaponization of college credentials shows how merit can become a kind of tyranny."[7]

While measures are in place to deal with the issue of overeducation, higher education institutions around the world need to do their part. It should be the case where the key competency to acquire is about how good one is able to accomplish complex goals both in the personal and professional life. What education should provide is the opportunity for change and the prospect of change for the better. Through education, one can raise his own intellectual power, moral, and personal standards, to allow the person to examine and muster issues carefully with more than one point of view, to deal with complex issues and develop a sense of community to realize the potential in all of us. HEIs can do their part by monitoring students' intellect and imagination, not by giving more assignments or demanding more learning hours from students that are pointless and unnecessary. It is not about how much facts one can churn out but about injecting curiosity into the minds. It is not about how much students cover in class but about what students discover through education.

It is heartening to note that some institutions are offering courses to develop global citizenship among the students. For example, International Baccalaureate requires students to complete a learner profile, a document that focuses on the students' personal qualities such as communication,

---

[6] For more on this, see Allport, "*The Nature of Prejudice.*"
[7] Sandel, "*The Tyranny of Merit,*" p. 85.

thinking, knowledge, caring, and risk taking. In a report commissioned by the Australian Education Council, a proposal was put forth to incorporate the Australian Tertiary Admission Rank (ATAR)—a score for universities to determine students' academic performance—with a learner profile, which captures students' extra-curricular activities such as part-time work, sports, hobbies, and engagement with society.[8]

Certainly, the effects of digital technology are not to be ignored. The proliferation of information and technology has created learning opportunities as well as challenges. Technology has shortened our attention spans and overwhelmed our brain with a universe of information. It is worth noting that concerns about information overload are not new. Writing emerged some 5,000 years ago in the Sumerian City of Uruk (now Southern Iraq) precisely because of the need to keep track with the vast amount of transactions in the city that was active in commercial trade.

The fact is there is a limit to how much we can absorb and understand. The human genome consists of about 750 megabytes, which is the size of a small USB. It is impossible for humans to digest the vast amount of information that is out there. How much information can we absorb? Consider this example.[9] Typically, to understand what one speaks, we need to process 60 bits of information per second. We have a processing limit of 120 bits of information per second that means we can hardly understand two or more people talking to us at the same time. Our brain can switch into mind-wandering mode (daydreaming) that differs from the state when we are paying attention to say reading a book or writing an essay. There are therefore two brain states, when one is active and the other is not. One state can distract the other. Suppose you are reading a book, the mind-wandering state takes over. You start to think of all other things except the contents of what you are reading. It is only when we are attentive, we can think of something creative.[10]

---

[8] See O'Connell, Milligan, and Bentley, "*Beyond ATAR.*"
[9] As told in Levitin, "*The Organised Mind,*" p. 13.
[10] We are fed with so much information—from the appearance of the printing press, television, and smartphones—which kept us busier than ever before. And we are doing more work than before. Things that we can expect service companies' staff to do for us, we are now expected to do them ourselves. We are expected

Institutions of higher learning can help to improve our ability to learn, to navigate the vast space of data, and to monitor our errors. Below are some of the key takeaways on teaching and learning for educators and HEIs.

First, the task of educators is to understand their students, taking into account their goals and interests. Educators should make sure that their students are neither too overwhelmed nor too bored by the course materials presented to them. With goals and a range of activities that matches students' skills and passion, students can concentrate on the activities, find them enjoyable, and feel that time flies.

Second, educators should stimulate the students' imagination with relevant stories and analogues and give them the opportunity to explore what interests them and what they believe in. In the traditional educational system, students are scared of being wrong. They do not receive credit for wanting to learn more and learning something that is not on the tests. Students lose interest in learning when curiosity is punished. Imagine a student who participates in class and asks questions and being punished or reprimanded for disturbing the class. The student will quickly learn to temper his curiosity drive and stop participating in class. Great teachers encourage their students to go deeper and avoid giving negative feedback responses.

Third, HEIs should recognize that it is not possible to establish the state of effective learning if going to school is seen as a chore. Sadly,

---

to check-in our reservations, book the seat, and obtain the boarding pass via the airline companies' websites; tasks that used to be done by the airline employees. At fast food restaurants, we are expected to order our food using the machine rather than directly placing orders with the employees at the counter. We scan our purchases in the supermarkets, pump our own gas at petrol stations, access websites to retrieve forms, pay bills (e.g., for banking and mobile phone services), and doing the work that were done by the employees. With smartphones, messages and notification alerts and the corresponding hypertexts are constantly appearing on the screen. The senders demand almost immediate attention from us, arising from the social expectation that any unanswered messages are the sign of disrespect to the sender. Together, we have a recipe for addiction. Indeed, we can be so absorbed with our smartphones and social media accounts or information in this context that we sometimes withdraw from others.

the meritocratic arms race creates such an environment—high stress and anxiety driven. A majority of students have no insight into other purpose of education other than to obtain a qualification that enables them to get a job, the ends of their actions. HEIs should strive to change the mindset, to use school years as a time to think, explore and reflect on what is worth caring about. HEIs should set up an environment in which students gain satisfaction through learning to train their students freely and intelligently not just for work. School is like a garden. In a garden, it is easy, by process of neglect, to ruin the food crops and plants. Likewise, students are delicate, and interests and passion so numerous and far reaching that their sentiments to the school and education can be dangerously misdirected. Students can be adapted to the school, if they are properly cared for, guided, and nurtured. When going to school is a joy, learning is easier.

Fourth, HEIs should review the single discipline solution to a multidisciplinary approach. Employers and educators have advised HEIs to step out of specialization and take up multidisciplinary courses. We hear of a great deal of challenges arising from overspecializing, confining our knowledge to a narrow compartment, and leaning to the emergence of two cultures—sciences and humanities—which are separate and sometimes hostile to each other. Any within disciplines are unable or unwilling to say anything to the other. The problem is that in the university, students are forced to choose without having at their disposal the kind of knowledge that would enable them to acquire cross-disciplinary knowledge. Even when students are allowed to read other courses, there are often prescribed by the college. Prescribing Chemistry for History students or History for Chemistry students does not equate to prescribing the interest in the subject. It is more pertinent for cross-fertilization of different disciplines to take place by giving generous allowance of time for the people of varying interest of socialize and explore each other's mind. The delivery of cross-disciplinary courses has to be thought through carefully to make the effort worthwhile.

Fifth, teaching facts and theories are no longer enough. The complexity of the world means that one has to consider broader implications and consideration, including economic, political, social, cultural, technological, and emotional factors. For teaching of science, for examples, facts and theories should be questioned and tested with data collected by students themselves. Students should be encouraged to question every fact and theory and consider the human side of science and the broader implication of science on the society.[11] It is not about teaching the subjects. Great teachers teach students, engaging and enthusing students by creating conditions in which students will want to learn and enabling them by provoking students so that they are inspired to explore further, not by offering answers to questions they have not asked.

Sixth, schools and educators should dispense with old school mindset of passive learning as they approach the information and technology age. HEIs should consider new teaching pedagogies such as the use of discussion groups, peer assessment, using social media, and feedback opportunities with prerecorded material. The best teaching model schools is a hybrid one that allows for social interaction and physical engagement and puts value into virtual learning and digital literacy.

Seventh, HEIs should get their students to experience "flow." To do so, as Mihaly Csikszentmihalyi told us, the educators must get their students to merge actions and awareness and to step into the situation where the actor and actions become one.[12] Students ought to feel that his or her skills are fully engaged by challenges. This is when "the student feels when he thinks he has found the solution to a difficult problem"—a good match between the student's ability and skills and the challenge posed by the problem.[13] The other element of the flow experience relates to knowing what the students are trying to achieve. With clear goals, there can be

---

[11] See Tang, *Teach Questions, Not Answers.*

[12] In *Literacy and Intrinsic Motivation,* Mihaly Csikszentmihalyi argued that the chief obstacles to literacy is not cognitive, but the drive and motivation to learn. "It is not that students cannot learn; it is that they do not wish to." And if educators invest only a fraction of the resources on trying to transmit information—by devising new models of learning, new methods of instruction and new teaching technologies—we could achieve much better results. Csikszentmihalyi, "*Literacy and Intrinsic Motivation,*" p. 115.

[13] Ibid., p. 128.

meaningful feedback and with knowledge of whether students are doing well or not, it becomes easier for them to maintain involvement.

Universities are confounded with multiple objectives; to be a leader in scientific research, to excel in teaching, to provide the best learning experience to students, and the mission dictates the allocation of resources and policies administered by the higher education institution. In these difficult times, universities have to compete fiercely for students domestically and internationally. More will decide to move their program online, allowing them to reach millions via pin-sharp video and, in no time, 3D holograms. With online education, ancient chores like marking exams and classifying students will be done by computers. Cost savings from online provision are passed on to consumers, resulting in thousands of weaker universities to close as students discover than they can get better value for money from taking online education. It is a mistake for HEIs to err on the side of caution and do nothing. They should adapt to the change quickly and do something to meet new demands and new markets.

References

Acemoglu, D., and J. Robinson. 2020. *The Narrow Corridor: States, Societies, and the Fate of Liberty.* New York, NY: Penguin Books.

Adams, C. 2019. *The Six Secrets of Intelligence: What Your Education Failed to Teach You.* London: Icon Books Ltd.

Akerlof, G. 1970. "The Market for Lemons: Quality Uncertainty and the Market Mechanism." *Quarterly Journal of Economics* 84, pp. 353–374.

Alexander, P.A. 2019. "Seeking Common Ground: Surveying the Theoretical and Empirical Landscapes for Curiosity and Interest." *Educational Psychology Review* 31, pp. 897–904.

Allen, R.E. 1991. *Greek Philosophy: Thales to Aristotle,* 3rd ed. New York, NY: The Free Press.

Allport, G. 1954. *The Nature of Prejudice.* Reading: Addition-Wesley.

Anderson, C.A., and B.J. Bushman. 2001. "Effects of Violent Video Games on Aggressive Behavior, Aggressive Cognition, Aggressive Affect, Psychological Arousal, and Prosocial Behavior: A Meta-Analytic Review of the Scientific Literature." *Psychological Science* 12, pp. 353–359.

Anderson, C.A., D.A. Gentile, and K.E. Buckley. 2007. *Violent Video Game Effects on Children and Adolescents.* New York, NY: Oxford University Press.

Aoun, J.E. 2018. *Robot-Proof: Higher Education in the Age Of Artificial Intelligence.* Cambridge: MIT Press.

Arendt, H. 1961. *Between Past and Future.* London: Faber and Faber.

Arenson, K.W. 2004. "Is It Grade Inflation, or are Students Just Smarter?" *New York Times,* www.nytimes.com/2004/04/18/weekinreview/is-it-grade-inflation-or-are-students-just-smarter.html (accessed April 18, 2004).

Arin, K. 2019. "Too Much Time on Smartphone Poses Health Threat." *Korean Herald,* www.koreaherald.com/view.php?ud=20191118000889 (accessed November 18, 2019).

Arum, R., and J. Roksa. 2010. *Academically Adrift: Limited Learning on College Campuses.* Chicago: University of Chicago Press.

Autor, D. 2014. "Skills, Education, and the Rise of Earnings Inequality Among the 'Other 99 Percent'." *Science* 344, pp. 843–851.

Baggini, J. 2012. *The Ego Trick: What Does it Mean to be You.* London: Granta.

Baggini, J. 2019. *How the World Thinks: A Global History of Philosophy.* London: Granta.

Baldwin, R. 2019. *The Globotics Upheaval: Globalisation, Robotics and the Future of Work.* London: Weidenfeld and Nicolson.

Bastid, M. 1988. *Educational Reform in Early 20th Century China*. Ann Arbor: Centre for Chinese Studies, The University of Michigan.

BBC News. 2015. "College Payments Halted Amid Fraud Allegations." *BBC News*, www.bbc.com/news/uk-wales-34946835 (accessed November 27, 2015).

BBC News. 2015. "Police Talking to Welch Government Over College Fraud." *BBC News*, www.bbc.com/news/uk-wales-politics-34979325 (accessed December 02, 2015).

Beeson, J. 2015. *Leaning by Doing: The Real Connection Between Innovation, Wages, and Wealth*. New Haven: Yale University Press.

Bernasconi, A. 2013. "The Profit Motive in Higher Education." *International Higher Education* 71, pp. 8–10.

Blair, A. 2010. *Too Much to Know: Managing Scholarly Information Before the Modern Age*. New Haven: Yale University Press.

Bloom, B. 1984. "The 2 Sigma Problem: The Search for Methods of Group Instruction as Effective as One-to-One Tutoring." *Educational Researcher* 13, no. 6, pp. 4–16.

Blue, A. 2020. "5 Things we Know About the Jobs of the Future." *World Economic Forum*, www.weforum.org/agenda/2020/01/future-jobs-and-skills-in-demand/ (accessed January 24, 2020).

Blum, S. 2009. *My Word! Plagiarism and College Culture*. Ithaca: Cornell University Press.

Blum, S. 2016. *'I Love Learning. I Hate School': An Anthropology of College*. Ithaca: Cornell University Press.

Boden, M. 2018. *Artificial Intelligence: A Very Short Introduction*. Oxford: Oxford University Press.

Bok, D. 2013. *Higher Education in America*. New Jersey, NJ: Princeton University Press.

Brandon, C. 2010. *The Five-Year Party: How Colleges Have Given Up on Educating Your Child and What You Can Do About It*. Dallas: Benbella Books.

Brown, P., H. Lauder., and D. Ashton. 2011. *The Global Auction: The Broken Promises of Education, Jobs and Incomes*. New York, NY: Oxford University Press.

Browne, J. 2020. *Make, Think, Imagine: Engineering the future of civilisation*. London: Bloomsbury Publishing PLC.

Bryman, A. 2007. "Effective Leadership in Higher Education: A Literature Review." *Studies in Higher Education* 32, no. 6, pp. 693–710.

Burns, D.D. 1999. *Feeling Good: The New Mood Therapy*. New York, NY: Harper.

Cameron, N. 2017. *Will Robots Take Your Job?* Cambridge: Polity Press.

Carey, K. 2015. *The End of College: Creating the Future of learning and the University of Everywhere*. New York, NY: Riverhead Books.

Carr, N. 2011. *The Shallows: What the Internet Is Doing to Our Brains*. New York, NY: W.W. Norton and Company.

Carr, N. 2016. *Utopia Is Creepy and Other Provocations*. New York, NY: W.W. Norton and Company.

Carroll, A.B. 1995. "Stakeholder Thinking in Three Models of Management: A Perspective With Strategic Implications." In *Understanding Stakeholder Thinking*, ed. Nasi, J. Helsinki: LSR-Publications.

Case, A., and A. Deaton. 2020. *Deaths of Despair and the Future of Capitalism*. New Jersey, NJ: Princeton University Press.

Chakravorty, S. 2001. "The Trouble With Too Much Information." *MIT Sloan Management Review*, https://sloanreview.mit.edu/article/the-trouble-with-too-much-information/ (accessed September 21, 2001).

Ciulla, J.B. 2001. "Carving Leaders From the Warped Wood of Humanity." *Canadian Journal of Administrative Sciences* 18, no. 4, pp. 313–319.

Clark, A.E., S. Fleche, R. Layard, N. Powdthavee, and G. Ward. 2018. *The Origins of Happiness: The Science of Well-Being Over the Life Course*. New Jersey, NJ: Princeton University Press.

Coe, R., C. Aloisi, S. Higgins, and L.E. Major. 2014. *What Makes Great Teaching? Review of the Underpinning Research*. Centre for Evaluation and Monitoring: Durham University and the Sutton Trust.

Cohen, B. 2018. *Post-Capitalist Entrepreneurship: Startups for the 99%*. New York, NY: CRC Press.

College of St. Scholastica. 2015. "Is a Liberal Education Still Relevant? Research Says 'Yes!'", www.css.edu/the-sentinel-blog/is-a-liberal-education-relevant-.html (accessed October 05, 2015).

Collini, S. 2018. *Speaking of Universities*. London: Verso.

Common Sense Media. 2015. *The Common Sense Media Census: Media Use by Tweens and Teens*. San Francisco: Common Sense Media, Inc. www.commonsensemedia.org/sites/default/files/uploads/research/census_researchreport.pdf.

Creemers, B.P.M., and L. Kyriakides. 2006. "Critical Analysis of the Current Approaches to Modelling Educational Effectiveness: The Importance of Establishing a Dynamic Model." *School Effectiveness and School Improvement* 17, pp. 347–366.

Csikszentmihalyi, M. 1990. "Literacy and Intrinsic Motivation." *Daedalus* 119, no. 2, pp. 115–140.

Cszszentmihalyi, M. 1990. *Flow: The Psychology of Optimal Experience*. New York, NY: HarperPerennial.

Cutler, D., and L. Summers. 2020. "The COVID-19 Pandemic and the $16 Trillion Virus." *Journal of American Medical Association*, Viewpoint, https://jamanetwork.com/journals/jama/fullarticle/2771764 (accessed October 12, 2020).

Danielson, C. 2007. *Enhancing Professional Practice: A Framework for Teaching*. Alexandria: Association For Supervision And Curriculum Development.

Davidson, C. 2017. *The New Education: How to Revolutionize the University to Prepare Students for a World in Flux.* New York, NY: Basic Books.

De Boer, H., and L. Goedegebuure. 2009. "The Changing Nature of the Academic Deanship." *Leadership* 5, no. 3, pp. 347–364.

De Onzono, S.I. 2011. *The Learning Curve: How Business Schools are Re-Inventing Education.* Hampshire: Palgrave MacMillan.

De Pree, M. 1989. *Leadership is an Art.* New York, NY: Doubleday.

Dean, P.J. 1997. "Dale Brethower: The Knowledge Base of human Performance Technology." In *Performance Improvement Pathfinders: Models for Organizational Learning Systems,* ed. Dean, P.J., and Ripley, D.E. Washington DC: ISPI.

Deci, E. 1971. "Effects of Externally Mediated Rewards on Intrinsic Motivation." *Journal of Personality and Social Psychology* 18, pp. 105–115.

Delaney, K. 2017. "The Robot That Takes Your Job Should Pay Taxes, Says Bill Gates." *Quartz,* https://qz.com/911968/bill-gates-the-robot-that-takes-your-job-should-pay-taxes/ (accessed February 17, 2017).

Dewey, J. 1967. "My Pedagogic Creed." In *Dewey on Education,* edited by Dworkin, M. New York, NY: Teachers College Press.

Dewey, J. 1916. *Democracy and Education.* Hollywood FL: Simon and Brown.

McDermott, J. 2016. "A Class Apart." *The Economist,* www.economist.com/1843/2017/07/18/a-class-apart (accessed March 19, 2016).

Edsall, T.B. 2018. "Robots Can't Vote, But they Helped Elect Trump." *New York Times,* www.nytimes.com/2018/01/11/opinion/trump-robots-electoral-college.html (accessed January 11, 2018).

Enders, J., H. De Boer, and E. Weyer. 2013. "Regulatory Autonomy and Performance: The Reform of Higher Education Re-Visited." *Higher Education* 65, pp. 5–23.

Entrepreneur. 2016. "Sam Walton: Bargain Basement Billionaire." www.entrepreneur.com/article/197560 (accessed March 24, 2016).

Ezell, A., and J. Bear. 2012. *Degree Mills: The Billion-Dollar Industry That Has Sold Over a Million Fake Diplomas.* New York, NY: Prometheus Books.

Ferguson, C. 2010. "The Influence of Television and Video Game Use on Attention and School Problems: A Multivariate Analysis with Other Risk Factors Controlled." *Journal of Psychiatric Research* 45, no. 6, pp. 808–813.

Ferguson, C. 2015. "Do Angry Birds Make for Angry Children? A Meta-Analysis of Video Game Influences on Children's and Adolescents' Aggression, Mental Health, Prosocial Behavior, and Academic Performance." *Perspectives on Psychological Science* 10, no. 5, pp. 646–666.

Fombrun, C.J. 1996. *Reputation: Realizing Value from the Corporate Image.* Boston: Harvard Business School Press.

Fort, T.C., J.R. Pierce, and P.K, Schott. 2018. "New Perspectives on the Decline of US Manufacturing Employment." *Journal of Economic Perspectives* 32, no. 2, pp. 47–72.

Freud, S. 2019. *The Best of Sigmund Freud*. London: Popular.
Frey, C.B., and M.A. Osborne. 2015. *The Future of Employment: How Susceptible Are Jobs to Computerization?* Oxford: Oxford Martin School.
Friedman, T. 2014. "How to Get a Job at Google." *New York Times*, www.nytimes.com/2014/02/23/opinion/sunday/friedman-how-to-get-a-job-at-google.html (accessed February 22, 2014).
Furedi, F. 2009. *Wasted: Why Education Isn't Educating*. London: Continuum.
Furedi, F. 2015. *Power of Reading: From Socrates to Twitter*. London: Bloomsbury.
Gabriel, Z. 2004. *So Many Books: Reading and Publishing in an Age of Abundance*. London: Paul Dry Books.
Gada, K. 2021. *ATOM: It is Time to Upgrade the Economy*, 2nd ed. New York, NY: Business Express Press, LLC.
Gardner, J.W. 1961. *Excellence: Can we be Equal and Excellent Too?* New York, NY: Harper.
Gee, J.P. 2003. *What Video Games Have to Teach us About Learning and Literacy*. New York, NY: Palgrave MacMillan.
Gentile, D.A., E.L. Swing, C.G. Lim, and A. Khoo. 2012. "Videogames Playing, Attention Problems, and Impulsiveness: Evidence of Bidirectional Causality." *Psychology of Popular Media Culture* 1, no. 1, pp. 62–70.
George A. 2017. *You can do Anything: The Surprising Power of a 'Useless' Liberal Arts Education*. New York, NY: Back Bay Books.
Gneezy, U., and J. List. 2013. *The Why Axis: Hidden Motives and the Undiscovered Economics of Everyday Life*. New York, NY: Random House Business Books.
Goldin, C., and L. Katz. 2008. *The Race Between Education and Technology*. Cambridge, Mass: Belknap Press of Harvard University Press.
Goody, J. 2006. *The Thief of History*. Cambridge: Cambridge University Press.
Gordon, R.J. 2018. "Declining American Economic Growth Despite Ongoing Innovation." *Explorations in Economic History* 69, pp. 1–12.
Grant, A. 2021. *Think Again: The Power of Knowing What You Don't Know*. New York, NY: Viking.
Green, A. 2015. "Will Corinthian Colleges be Able to Payback Students?" *The Atlantic*, www.theatlantic.com/education/archive/2015/10/corinthian-colleges-pay-back-students/413227/ (accessed October 30, 2015).
Greenfield, S. 2015. *Mind Change: How Digital Technologies are Leaving their Mark on Our Brains*. New York, NY: Random House.
Greenleaf, R.K. 2001. *Servant Leadership: A Journey into the Nature of Legitimate Power and Greatness*. New York, NY: Paulist Press.
Greenspan, A., and A. Wooldridge. 2018. *Capitalism in America: An Economic History of the United States*. New York, NY: Allen Lane.
Gregorutti, G., O. Espinoza, L.E. Gonzales, and J. Loyola. 2016. "What If Privatizing Higher Education Becomes an Issue? The Case of Chile and Mexico." *Compare: A Journal of Comparative and International Education* 46, no. 1, pp. 136–158.

Guessoum, N., and A. Osama. 2015. "Revive Universities of the Muslim World." *Nature* 526, pp. 634–636.

Guilbault, M. 2016. "Students As Customers in Higher Education: Reframing The Debate." *Journal of Marketing for Higher Education* 26, no. 2, pp. 132–142.

Guilbault, M. 2018. "Students As Customers in Higher Education: The (Controversial) Debate Needs to End." *Journal of Retailing and Consumer Services* 40, pp. 295–298.

Gupta, A. 2008. "International Trends and Private Higher Education in India." *International Journal of Educational Management* 22, no. 6, pp. 565–594.

Hacker, A., and C. Dreifus. 2010. *Higher Education? How Colleges are Wasting Our Money and Failing Our Kids – And What We Can do About it*. New York, NY: Times Books.

Harari, Y.N. 2018. *21 Lessons for the 21st Century*. London: Jonathan Cape.

Harman, G. 2003. "Australian Academics and Prospective Academics: Adjustment to a More Commercial Environment." *Higher Education Management and Policy* 15, pp. 105–122.

Harris, S. 2012. *Free Will*. New York, NY: Free Press.

Hawking, S. 2016. "This Is the Most Dangerous Times For Our Planet." *The Guardian*, www.theguardian.com/commentisfree/2016/dec/01/stephen-hawking-dangerous-time-planet-inequality (accessed December 01, 2016).

Hayek, F.A. 1945. "The Use of Knowledge in Society." *American Economic Review* 35, no. 4, pp. 519–530.

Herlily, V., A. Anhar, Y. Ahda, and R. Sumarmin. 2018. "Application of Learning Model Learning Guided Discovery With Scientific Approach to Enhance Learning Competency Science Seventh Grade Students." *International Journal of Progressive Sciences and Technologies* 6, no. 2, pp. 499–505.

Hirchman, A. 2013. *The Passions and the Interests: Political Arguments for Capitalism Before its Triumph*. New Jersey, NJ: Princeton University Press.

Hirsch, E.D. 1999. *The Schools We Need and Why We Don't Have Them*. New York, NY: Anchor Books.

Howard, J. 2019. "When Kids Get their First Cell Phones Around the World." https://edition.cnn.com/2017/12/11/health/cell-phones-for-kids-parenting-without-borders-explainer-intl/index.html (Accessed June 17, 2019).

Howard, R.M. 1999. *Standing in the Shadow of Giants: Plagiarism, Authors, Collaborators*. Stamford, Conn: Ablex.

IPSOS. 2020. "Higher Education: In-Person or Online? 29-Country IPSOS Survey Conducted for the World Economic Forum." www.ipsos.com/sites/default/files/ct/news/documents/2020-11/higher-education-in-person-or-online.pdf (accessed November 2020).

Isaacson, W. 2014. *The Innovators*. New York, NY: Simon & Schuster.

Jeong, H. 2012. "A Comparison of the Influence of Electronic Books and Paper Books on Reading Comprehension, Eye Fatigue, and Perception." *Electronic Library* 39, no. 3, pp. 390–408.

Johnson, V. 2003. *Grade Inflation: A Crisis in College Education*. New York, NY: Springer.

Josey, A. 2012. *Lee Kuan Yew: The Crucial Years (1959 –1970)*. Singapore: Marshall Cavendish Editions.

Kahneman, D. 2011. *Thinking, Fast and Slow*. London: Allen Lane.

Katsikas, A. 2015. "Same Performance, Better Grades." *The Atlantic*, www.theatlantic.com/education/archive/2015/01/same-performance-better-grades/384447/ (accessed January 13, 2015).

Kerr, C. 1963. *The Uses of the University*. Cambridge: Harvard University Press.

Keynes, J.M. 1933. *Essays in Persuasion*. New York, NY: Norton.

Kilpatrick, W.H. 1926. *Foundations of Method: Informal Talks on Teaching*. New York, NY: The MacMillan Company.

Kinser, K. 2013. "The Quality-Profit Assumption." *International Higher Education* 71, pp. 12–13.

Koris, R., and P. Nokelainen. 2015. "The Student-Customer Orientation Questionnaire (SCOQ): Application of Customer Metaphor to Higher Education." *International Journal of Educational Management* 29, no. 10, pp. 115–138.

Koris, R., A. Ortenblad, K. Kerem, and T. Ojala. 2015. "Student-Customer Orientation at a Higher Education Institution: The Perspectives of Undergraduate Business Students." *Journal of Marketing for Higher Education* 25, no. 1, pp. 29–44.

Kouzes, J.M., and B.Z. Poster. 1993. *Credibility: How Leaders Gain and Lose It*. San Francisco: Jossey-Bass.

Krugman, P. 1997. "The Accidental Theorist." *Slate Magazine*, https://slate.com/business/1997/01/the-accidental-theorist.html (accessed January 24, 1997).

LaBelle, J., and D. Jendall. 2016. "Characteristics of Jesuit Colleges and Universities in the United States: A Reciprocal Interdependence Analysis." *Journal of Catholic Education* 19, no. 3, pp. 264–288.

Larson, Q. 2017. "A Warning From Bill Gates, Elon Musk, and Stephen Hawking." www.freecodecamp.org/news/bill-gates-and-elon-musk-just-warned-us-about-the-one-thing-politicians-are-too-scared-to-talk-8db9815fd398/ (accessed February 18, 2017).

Lechuga, V.M. 2008. "Assessment, Knowledge, and Customer Service: Contextualizing Faculty Work at For-Profit Colleges And Universities." *The Review of Higher Education* 31, no. 3, pp. 287–307.

Levitin, D. 2014. *The Organised Mind: Thinking Straight in the Age of Information Overload.* London: Viking.

Levy, D.C. 2006. "The Unanticipated Explosion: Private Higher Education's Global Surge." *Comparative Education Review* 50, no. 2, pp. 217–240.

Lin, Y.C., and Y.K Toh. 2017. "People in Singapore Spend Over 12 Hours on Gadgets Daily: Survey." *The Straits Times*, www.straitstimes.com/singapore/12hr-42min-connected-for-hours (accessed April 03, 2017).

Liu, Z. 2005. "Reading Behaviour in the Digital Environment: Changes in Reading Behaviour Over the Past Ten Years." *Journal of Documentation* 61, no. 6, pp. 700–712.

Liu, Z. 2012. "Digital Reading: An Overview." *Chinese Journal of Library and Information Science* 5, no. 1, pp. 85–94.

Lok, B.T., A. Gazi Mahabubul, and I. Abdul Rahman. 2016. "Balancing Managerial and Academic Values: Mid-Level Academic Management at a Private University in Malaysia." *International Journal of Educational Management* 30, no. 2, pp. 308–322.

Longden, B., and C. Belanger. 2013. "Universities: Public Good or Private Profit." *Journal of Higher Education Policy and Management* 35, no. 5, pp. 501–522.

Lusch, R., and C. Wu. 2012. "A Service Science Perspective on Higher Education: Linking Service Productivity Theory and Higher Education Reform." Centre for American Progress, www.americanprogress.org/issues/education-postsecondary/reports/2012/08/13/11972/a-service-science-perspective-on-higher-education/ (accessed August 2012).

Lynham. S.A., and T.J. Chermack. 2006. "Responsible Leadership for Performance: A Theoretical Model and Hypotheses." *Journal of Leadership and Organizational Studies* 12, no. 4, pp. 73–88.

Maak, T., and N.M. Pless. 2006. "Responsible Leadership in a Stakeholder Society: A Relational Perspective." *Journal of Business Ethics* 66, pp. 99–115.

Mangen, A., B.R. Walgermo, and K. Bronnick. 2013. "Reading Linear Texts on Paper Versus Computer Screen: Effects on Reading Comprehension." *International Journal of Educational Research* 58, pp. 61–68.

Marks, D. 2007. "The Unsettled Meaning of Undergraduate Education in a Competitive Higher Education Environment." *Higher Education in Europe* 32, pp. 173–183.

Maslow, A.H. 1971. *The Farther Reaches of Human Nature.* New York, NY: Penguin Books.

McCurry, J. 2010. "Internet Addiction Driving South Koreans Into Realms of Fantasy." *The Guardian*, www.theguardian.com/world/2010/jul/13/internet-addiction-south-korea (accessed July 13, 2010).

McLuhan, M. 1994. *Understanding Media: The Extensions of Men.* Cambridge: MIT Press.

Mincer, J. 1974. *Schooling, Experience and Earnings.* New York, NY: Columbia University Press.

Ministry of Education, Singapore. 2020. "Blended Learning to Enhance Schooling Experience and Further Develop Students into Self-Directed Learners." Singapore Ministry of Education. www.moe.gov.sg/news/press-releases/20201229-blended-learning-to-enhance-schooling-experience-and-further-develop-students-into-self-directed-learners (accessed December 29, 2020).

Mintzberg, H. 2005. *Managers Not MBAs: A Hard Look at the Soft Practice of Managing and Management Development.* San Francisco: Berrett-Koehler Publishers, Inc.

Mlodinow, L. 2012. *Subliminal: How Your Unconscious Mind Rules your Behavior.* New York, NY: Pantheon Books.

Molina, B. 2017. "When Is the Right Age to Buy Your Child a Smartphone?" *USA Today*, www.usatoday.com/story/tech/talkingtech/2017/08/24/when-right-age-buy-your-child-smartphone-wait-until-8-th/593195001/ (accessed August 24, 2017).

Montez, J. M., M. Wolverton, and W. Gmelch. 2002. "The Roles and Challenges of Deans." *The Review of Higher Education* 26, no. 2, pp. 241–266.

Nasiripour, S. 2015. "Obama to Cancel Debts Owned By Defrauded For-Profit College Students." *The Huffington Post*, www.huffpost.com/entry/student-debt-for-profit-colleges_n_56607635e4b079b2818d7c7a (accessed December 03, 2015).

Newman, J.H. 1996. *The Idea of a University.* New Haven: Yale University Press.

Nisbett, R.E. 2019. *The Geography of Thought: How Asians and Westerners Think Differently.* London: Nicholas Brealey Publishing.

Nussbaum, M. 2010. *Not For Profit: Why Democracy Needs the Humanities.* New Jersey, NJ: Princeton University Press.

O'Connell, M., S. Milligan, and T. Bentley. 2019. *Beyond ATAR: A Proposal For Change.* Victoria: Koshland Innovation Fund.

Oakley, B., and T. Sejnowski (with McConville, A.). 2018. *Learning How to Learn: How to Succeed in School Without Spending All Your Time Studying.* New York, NY: A TeacherPerigee Book.

Oppenheimer, A. 2019. *The Robots are Coming: The Future of Jobs in the Age of Automation.* New York, NY: Vintage Books.

Oxfam. 2014. "Children and Parents: Media Use and Attitudes Report 2018." www.ofcom.org.uk/__data/assets/pdf_file/0027/76266/childrens_2014_report.pdf (accessed October 2014).

Ozdem-Yilmaz, Y., and K. Bilican. 2020. "Discovery Learning - Jerome Bruner." In *Science Education in Theory and Practice,* ed. Akpan, B. and T.J. Kennedy, Cham: Springer.

Palmer, P.J. 2007. *The Courage to Teach: Exploring the Inner Landscape of a Teacher's Life*. CA: John Wiley and Sons.

Paranto, S., and M. Kelkar. 1999. "Employer Satisfaction With Job Skills of Business College Graduates and Its Impact on Hiring Behavior." *Journal of Marketing for Higher Education* 9, no. 3, pp. 73–89.

Pavlou, V. 2006. "Pre-Adolescents' Perceptions of Competence, Motivation and Engagement in Art Activities." *International Journal of Art & Design Education* 35, no. 2, pp. 194–204.

Peterson, E.G., and S. Hidi. 2019. "Curiosity and Interest: Current Perspectives." *Educational Psychology Review* 31, pp. 781–788.

Pinker, S. 2018. *Enlightened Now: The Case for Reason, Science, Humanism, and Progress*. New York, NY: Viking.

Pintrich, P.R. 2003. "A Motivational Science Perspective on the Role of Student Motivation in Learning and Teaching Contexts." *Educational Psychology* 95, no. 4, pp. 667–686.

Pitcher, G.S. 2013. "Managing the Tensions Between Maintaining Academic Standards and the Commercial Imperative in a UK Private Sector Higher Education Institution." *Higher Education Policy and Management* 35, no. 4, pp. 421–431.

Postman, N. 1993. *Technopoly: The Surrender of Culture to Technology*. New York, NY: Vintage Books.

Postman, N. 1996. *The End of Education: Redefining the Value of School*. New York, NY: Vintage Books.

Prestridge, S., and C. De Aldama. 2016. "A Classification Framework for Exploring Technology-Enabled Practice: FrameTEP." *Journal of Educational Computing Research* 54, no. 7, pp. 901–921.

Priyadharshini, E., and A. Robinson-Pant. 2003. "The Attractions of Teaching: An Investigation Into Why People Change Careers to Teach." *Journal of Education for Teaching* 29, no. 2, pp. 95–112.

RAND. 2013. *Digital Leaning: Education and Skills in the Digital Age*. California: Rand Corporation. www.rand.org/pubs/conf_proceedings/CF369.html

Rezaeian, M. 2016. "Muslim World's Universities: Past, Present, and Future." *Middle East Journal of Family Medicine* 14, no. 7, pp. 39–41.

Reynolds, L., and N. Wilson. 1974. *Scribes and Scholars: A Guide to the Transmission of Greek and Latin Literature*. London: Oxford University Press.

Robinson, K. 2009. *The Element: How Finding Your Passion Changes Everything*. London: Penguin Books.

Robinson, K., and L. Aronica. 2018. *You, Your Child and School: Navigate Your Way to the Best Education*. London: Allen Lane.

Rogers, C. 2016. *On Becoming a Person: A Therapist's View of Psychotherapy*. London: Robinsons.

Roth, M.S. 2014. *Beyond the University: Why Liberal Education Matters*. New Haven: Yale University Press.

Rousseau, J.J. 2003. *Emile (Or Treatise on Education)*. New York, NY: Prometheus Books.

Sachs, J. 2005. *The End of Poverty: How We Can Make it Happen in Our Lifetime*. New York, NY: The Penguin Press.

Sachs, J. 2011. *The Price of Civilisation: Reawakening American Virtue and Prosperity*. New York, NY: Random House.

Safon, V. 2009. "Measuring the Reputation of Top US Business Schools: A MIMIC Modeling Approach." *Corporate Reputation Review* 12, no. 3, pp. 204–228.

Sakellariou, C. 2003. "Rates of Return to Investments in Formal and Technical/Vocational Education in Singapore." *Education Economics* 11, no. 1, pp. 73–87.

Sam, C.Y. 2017. *Private Education in Singapore: Contemporary Issues and Challenges*. Singapore: World Scientific.

Sandel, M. 2013. *What Money Can't Buy: The Moral Limits of Markets*. London: Penguin Books.

Sandel, M. 2020. *The Tyranny of Merit: What's Become of the Common Good*. New York, NY: Allen Lane.

Schein, E. 1992. *Organisational Culture and Leadership*. San Francisco: Jossey-Bass.

Sen, A. 2006. *The Argumentative Indian: Writing on Indian Cultures, History and Identity*. London: Penguin Books.

Shiller, R. 2019. *Narrative Economics: How Stories Go Viral and Drive Major Economic Events*. Princeton: Princeton University Press.

Shiller, R. 2019. "Narratives About Technology-Induced Job Degradation then and Now." *Journal of Policy Modeling* 41, pp. 477–488.

Skallerud, K. 2011. "School Reputation and its Relation to Parents' Satisfaction and Loyalty." *International Journal of Educational Management* 25, no. 7, pp. 671–686.

Sloman, S., and P. Fernbach. 2017. *The Knowledge Illusion: Why We Never Think Alone*. New York, NY: Riverhead Books.

Smith, A. 2000 (1776). *The Wealth of Nations*. New York, NY: The Modern Library.

Snow, C.P. 2017. *The Two Cultures*. Cambridge: Cambridge University Press.

Spence, M. 1974. *Market Signaling: Informational Transfer in Hiring and Related Process*. Cambridge: Harvard University Press.

Spence, M. 2011. "The Impact of Globalisation on Income and Employment: The Downside of Integrating Markets." *Foreign Affairs* 90, no. 4, pp. 28–41.

Spohrer, J., D. Fodell, and W. Murphy. 2012. "10 Reasons Service Science Matters to Universities." *EduCause Review.* https://er.educause.edu/articles/2012/11/ten-reasons-service-science-matters-to-universities (November/December 2012).

Susskind, R., and D. Susskind. 2015. *The Future of the Professions: How Technology Will Transform the Work of Human Experts.* Oxford: Oxford University Press.

Swing, E.L., D.A. Gentile, C.A. Anderson, and D.A. Walsh. 2010. "Television and Videogame Exposure and the Development of Attention Problem." *Pediatrics* 126, no. 2, pp. 214–221.

Tan, A.M. 2002. *Malaysian Private Higher Education: Globalization, Privatization, Transformation and Marketplaces.* London: ASEAN Academic Press, Ltd.

Tan, E.C. 2020. "Universities Need to Tear Down Subject Silos." *The Straits Times*, September 10, 2020.

Tan, T.Y. 2020. *The Idea of Singapore: Smallness Unconstrained.* Singapore: World Scientific.

Tang, K.S. 2020. "Teach Questions, Not Answers: Science Literacy Is a Crucial Skill." *The Conversation*, https://theconversation.com/teach-questions-not-answers-science-literacy-is-a-crucial-skill-144731 (accessed August 24, 2020).

Tham, S.Y. 2013. "Internationalizing Higher Education in Malaysia: Government Policies and University's Response." *Journal of Studies in International Education* 17, no. 5, pp. 648–662.

Tharoor, S. 2016. *Inglorious Empire: What the British Did to India.* London: C. Hurst & Co. Ltd.

The Guardian. 2020. "Most Children Own Mobile Phone by Age of Seven, Study Finds." *The Guardian*, www.theguardian.com/society/2020/jan/30/most-children-own-mobile-phone-by-age-of-seven-study-finds (accessed January 30, 2020).

Thiel, P. (with Masters, B.) 2014. *Zero to One: Notes on Startups, or How to Build the Future.* London: Virgin Books.

Toh, M.H., and C.S. Wong. 1999. "Rates of Return to Education in Singapore." *Education Economics* 7, no. 3, pp. 235–252.

Tooley, J. 2001. *The Global Education Industry: Lessons from Private Education in Developing Countries.* London: The Institute of Economic Affairs.

Twenge, J. 2017. *'iGen: Why Today's Super-Connected Kids are Growing Up Less Rebellious, More Tolerant and Less Happy—and Completely Unprepared for Adulthood.* New York: Atria Books.

Twenge, J. 2017. "How Smartphones Destroyed a Generation." *The Atlantic*, www.theatlantic.com/magazine/archive/2017/09/has-the-smartphone-destroyed-a-generation/534198/ (accessed September 2017).

UNESCO and OECD. 2005. *Guidelines for Quality Provision in Cross-Border Higher Education.* Paris: United Nations Educational, Scientific and Cultural Organization and the Organization for Economic Co-operation and Development.

Varaprasad, N. 2016. *50 Years of Technical Education in Singapore: How to Build a World Class TVET System.* Singapore: World Scientific.

Van de Meer, P., and R. Wielers. 1996. "Educational Credentials and Trust in the Labour Market." *Kyklos* 49, no. 1, pp. 29–46.

Vee, A. 2017. *Coding Literacy: How Computer Programming is Changing Writing.* Cambridge: The MIT Press.

Verhaest, D., and E. Verhofstadt. 2016. "Overeducation and Job Satisfaction: The Role of Job Demands and Control." *International Journal of Manpower* 37, no. 3, pp. 456–473.

Vidaver-Cohen, D. 2007. "Reputation Beyond the Rankings: A Conceptual Framework for Business School Research." *Corporate Reputation Review* 10, no. 4, pp. 278–304.

Ward, D. 2007. "Academic Values, Institutional Management, and Public Policies." *Higher Education Management and Policy* 19, p. 112.

Washburn, J. 2005. *University, Inc.: The Corporate Corruption of American Higher Education.* New York, NY: Basic Books.

Washington, B. 2019. "Industrial Education for the Negro (1903)." https://teachingamericanhistory.org/library/document/industrial-education-for-the-negro/ (accessed June 26, 2019).

Watson, R. 2010. *Future Minds: How the Digital Age Is Changing Our Minds, Why this Matters and What We Can do About It.* London: Nicholas Brealey Publishing.

Weiss, A. 1995. "Human Capital Vs. Signaling: Explanation of Wages." *Journal of Economic Perspectives* 9, no. 4, pp. 133–154.

Wiegel, M., and H. Gardner. 2009. "The Best of Both Literacies." *Educational Leadership* 66, no. 6, pp. 38–41.

Willetts, D. 2017. *A University Education.* Oxford: Oxford University Press.

Wolf, M. 2018. *Reader, Come Home: The Reading Brain in a Digital World.* New York, NY: Harper.

Wooldridge, A. 2005. *The Great Disruption: How Business is Coping with Turbulent Times.* New York, NY: Public Affairs.

World Economic Forum. 2020. "The Future of Jobs Report 2020." http://www3.weforum.org/docs/WEF_Future_of_Jobs_2020.pdf (accessed October 2020).

Yeo, K.Y., M.H. Toh, S.M. Thangavelu, and J. Wong. 2007. *Premium on Fields of Study: The Returns to Higher Education in Singapore.* Singapore: Singapore Centre for Applied and Policy Economics.

Zakaria, F. 2015. *In Defence of a Liberal Education*. New York, NY: W.W. Norton and Company.

Zakaria, F. 2020. *Ten Lessons for a Post-Pandemic World*. New York, NY: W.W. Norton and Company.

Zhao, X. 2016. "China has One in Five of All College Students in the World: Report." *China Daily*, www.chinadaily.com.cn/china/2016-04/08/content_24365038.htm (accessed April 04, 2016).

About the Author

Sam Choon-Yin, PhD, is the Dean at PSB Academy, Singapore, and the author of *Private Education in Singapore: Contemporary Issues and Challenges*. He graduated from the National University of Singapore (NUS), University of Technology, Sydney (UTS), and University of South Australia (UNISA) where he obtained his PhD in International Business and Management. His current research interests are in the field of international political economy and higher education policy. Aside from his responsibilities in teaching and research, Sam contributes as a member of the Academic Board at PSB Academy.

Index

academic
  integrity, 23, 127, 140
  leaders, 28
Acemoglu, D., 29, 39
Adams, C., 32–33
agency theory, 129–132
Amazon, 45
Anders, G., 44, 63
Aoun, J. E., 58
Aristotle, 1, 70, 71
artificial intelligence (AI), 37, 38, 42, 43, 52, 53, 59
Arum, R., 27
Ashesi University, 57, 58
ASPIRE, 40
assessment, 121
Australian Education Council, 150
Australian Tertiary Admission Rank (ATAR), 150

Baggini, J., 81
Bastid, M., 4
Bear, J., 22
Beeson, J., 43, 61
blended learning, 66, 67, 115
Bloom, B., 117
Blum, S., 26–27, 80–81, 99, 102
Boden, M., 43
Bok, D., 51
Boston International, 128
brain, 44, 87–89, 93, 100, 118–120
Brandon, C., 26
Browne, J., 42
Bruner, J., 102
Burns, D., 107

Cambridge University, 3
Cameron, N., 15
Camford Business School, 128
Carey, K., 27
Carr, N., 49, 76, 93, 99

Carroll, A., 135–137
Case, A., 39
Chakravorty, S., 97
Chermack, T., 135
Chile, 127–128
China, 3–4, 52
Chinese language, 112–113
Chomsky, N., 147, 148
Ciulla, J., 133
classroom, 121
  environment, 122
coding, 56, 60, 61
Cohen, B., 38
Cohen, M., 149
Collini, S., 79
Common Sense Media, 92
corporate social responsibility (CSR), 136
Council for Private Education (CPE), 130, 132
COVID-19, 114, 145, 147
credentials
  educational, 72
  for higher education, 28–33
  of university education, 21–28
Creemers, B., 121
cross-disciplinary courses, 54, 56, 152
Csikszentmihalyi, M., 75, 153
culture and learning, 90–91
Cutler, D., 145

Danielson, C., 122
Davidson, C., 57, 58
Deaton, A., 39
Deci, E., 80
De Onzono, S. I., 66–67
Dewey, J., 5–6
digitalization, 96
digital technology, 9, 47, 150
digitization, rise of, 9–15
diploma mills, 22, 23

172 INDEX

discovery-based learning, 101–102
discretionary/philanthropic responsibility, 136–137
Dreifus, C., 30, 31
Du Bois, W. E. B., 8

economic responsibility, 136
education
   economic purposes of, 7–9
   and religion, 2
   social purposes of, 5–7
educational effectiveness, 121
educational leaders, 28, 29, 144
Education Investment Corporation Limited (Educor), 143
Einstein, A., 13–14
Elliot, C., 8–9
employment, 38
   higher education institution, 129
   technology on, 39, 45–49
engineers, 55
Enron, 131
enthusiasm, 71
ethical responsibility, 137
externality, 6
Ezell, A., 22

Fee Protection Scheme (FPS), 130
Ford, H., 98
Freud, S., 118
Frey, C. B., 37
Furedi, F., 12–13, 72, 77, 94

Gabriel, Z., 95
Gada, K., 47
Gardner, J., 78
Gates, B., 37
Gee, J. P., 65
genuine intelligence, 43
Germany, 92
Gilded Age, 7
GitHub, 20, 33
Goody, J., 2
Google, 16, 19, 63, 101
Gordon, R., 42
Grant, A., 111
Greenspan, A., 21

Gutenberg, J., 95

Hacker, A., 30, 31
Hariri, Y. N., 42
Harris, S., 83
Hawking, S., 37, 44–45
Hayek, F. A., 24
Hierarchy of Needs Theory (Maslow), 85
higher education
   corporate social responsibility, 136
   in digital age, 53–68
   moral management in, 137–138
   postpandemic world, xi, xiv, 1, 15–17, 32, 145
   practices in, 126–129
higher education institutions (HEIs), 125, 126, 128–133, 136, 138, 140–142, 144, 146, 149, 152–154
Hirsch, E. D., 93, 116
Hisrchman, A., 70
homo sapiens, 71
human brain. *See* brain
Human Capital Theory, 84–85

IBM, 56
iGen, 108
India, 4
Industrial Revolution, 146
information technology, 59, 65
innovators, 8, 13–14
instruction, 122
International Baccalaureate, 149
Internet
   higher education, 101–105
   and learning ability, 91–97
   student performance and, 97–101
   technology and, 91–92, 116
Internet of Thing, 60
Interpretation of Dreams, The (Freud), 118
intrinsic learning, 78
IQ test, 133
Isaacson, W., 14
IT professionals, 54

Jeong, H., 97
Jesuits, 2, 10, 11, 137
Jobs, S., 14, 60

Kahneman, D., 90
Kelkar, M., 62
Kendal, D., 11
Kilpatrick, W. H., 74
Koris, R., 30
Krugman, P., 46–47
Kyriakides, L., 121

LaBelle, J., 11
Layard, R., 73
leadership, 133–134
    responsible, 134–144
learning
    blended, 66, 67, 115
    culture and, 90–91
    discovery-based, 101–102
    intrinsic, 78
    online, 15, 58, 66, 103, 114, 115
    See also passion for learning
learning ability, 88–91
    Internet and, 91–97
Learning Management System (LMS), 113, 114
legal responsibility, 136
liberal knowledge/liberal education, 6, 10–12
Liu, Z., 100
Luddites, 35
Lynham, S., 135

Maak, T., 134–135, 138
machine intelligence, 43–44
machines and computers, 36, 43, 44
Malaysia, 130–131
management of time, 121
Marx, K., 36
Maslow, A., 78, 85
McConville, A., 117–120
McLuhan, M., 96
Mexico, 127–128
Mincer, J., 84
Mintzberg, H., 21
Mlodinow, L., 44–45

monasteries, 2–4, 146
Morrill Act, 7
multidisciplinary approach, 1, 32, 54, 55, 57, 64, 67, 68, 116, 152
multitasking, 100
Musk, E., 37
Muslim world, 2

Nalanda, 4, 146
National Accreditation Board (NAB), 130
National Association of Colleges and Employers, 62
National Commission for Accreditation of Undergraduate Program (NAP), 131
National Institute of Technological Education of Argentina, 63
National University of Singapore (NUS), 57
neurodevelopmental function, 88, 89
neurons, 88
New International School of Thailand, 137
Newman, J. H., 5
news media, 54
Nisbett, R., 90–91, 112, 113
Northeastern University, 58, 59
Nozick, R., 111
Nussbaum, M., 11–13

Oakley, B., 117–120
Objectivo/UNIP, 137
online learning, 15, 58, 66, 103, 114, 115
orientation, 121
Osborne, M., 37

Palmer, P., 109–110
Paronto, S., 62
passionate learners, 70–73
passion for learning, 70, 73–76
    for higher education, 76–85
Pinker, S., 10, 71, 88
plagiarism, 27, 101, 140
Pless, N. M., 134–135, 138

Postman, N., 79, 95, 111
problem solving, 17, 42, 62, 64, 66, 88, 93, 99, 107, 129, 146
professional responsibilities, 122
profit-making education providers, 22, 23, 127
Program Consultants/Sales Executives, 132
public education institutions, 6, 23, 125

Quality Assurance Division (QAD), 131

relationship building, 138
Responsible Leadership for Performance (RLP), 135
Restrepo, P., 39
Reynolds, L., 1
Robinson, J., 29
Robinson, K., 115, 117
Roger, C., 104
Roksa, J., 27
Roth, M., 13
Rousseau, J.-J., 116

Sachs, J., 6, 69
Sandel, M., 149
Schmidt, E., 93
scientists, 13–14, 55, 88
Sejnowski, T., 117–120
self-actualization, 78
Service Science, Management and Engineering (SSME) initiative, 56
Shiller, R., 35
Signaling Theory, 33, 41, 51, 82, 84–85, 148
Singapore, 11, 57, 92, 115, 130, 132
Smith, A., 6, 70
Snow, C. P., 59
Society of Jesus. *See* Jesuits
South Korea, 91
Spence, M., 38, 84, 85
STEAM, 15
stewardship, 138
Sticht's Law, 94
structuring, 121

student-centric education institution, 29
student centricity, 142–143
Summers, L., 145
Susskind, D., 36
Susskind, R., 36

teachers
  effectiveness, 120–123
  great, 107, 109–120
teaching
  Danielson's framework for, 122
  modelling, 121
technology
  on employment, 45–49
  humans *vs.*, 41–45
  and Internet, 91–92, 116
  jobs and, 35–41
  rise of, 9–15
Tharoor, S., 4
Theil, P., 41
Thiel, P., 20–21
Tooley, J., 127
Trump, D., 149
trust, 19, 26, 32, 41, 44, 55, 148
T-shaped professionals, 56
Twenge, J., 20, 108

unemployment, 7, 35, 36
United Kingdom, 23, 92
United States, 5, 9, 11, 25, 27, 38, 57, 73, 91, 92, 125, 128
universities, early, 1–5
university administrators, 26, 129
university education, 1, 8, 9, 16, 19–29, 35, 41, 51–53, 62, 146
University of Bologna, 3
University of Karueein/University of al-Qarawiyyin, 2
University of Oxford, 3
US Department of Education, 128

Vee, A., 60
Virtual Learning Environments (VLEs), 110

Washington, B., 7
Welsh government, 23

westerners, 90, 91
West London Vocational Training Centre, 23
Willett, D., 3
Wilson, N., 1
Wolf, M., 89, 100, 102
Wooldridge, A., 21, 39

Wordsworth, W., 96
World Economic Forum, 52, 63, 114

Yahoo, 16

Zakaria, F., 11, 13, 31, 145
Zuckerberg, M., 11

OTHER TITLES IN THE COLLABORATIVE INTELLIGENCE COLLECTION

Jim Spohrer and Haluk Demirkan, Editors

- *How to Talk to Data Scientists* by Jeremy Elser
- *Leadership in The Digital Age* by Niklas Hageback
- *Cultural Science* by William Sims Bainbridge
- *The Future of Work* by Yassi Moghaddam, Heather Yurko, and Haluk Demirkan
- *Advancing Talent Development* by Philip Gardner and Heather N. Maietta
- *Virtual Local Manufacturing Communities* by William Sims Bainbridge
- *T-Shaped Professionals* by Yassi Moghaddam, Haluk Demirkan, and James Spohrer
- *The Interconnected Individual* by Hunter Hastings and Jeff Saperstein

Concise and Applied Business Books

The Collection listed above is one of 30 business subject collections that Business Expert Press has grown to make BEP a premiere publisher of print and digital books. Our concise and applied books are for…

- Professionals and Practitioners
- Faculty who adopt our books for courses
- Librarians who know that BEP's Digital Libraries are a unique way to offer students ebooks to download, not restricted with any digital rights management
- Executive Training Course Leaders
- Business Seminar Organizers

Business Expert Press books are for anyone who needs to dig deeper on business ideas, goals, and solutions to everyday problems. Whether one print book, one ebook, or buying a digital library of 110 ebooks, we remain the affordable and smart way to be business smart. For more information, please visit www.businessexpertpress.com, or contact sales@businessexpertpress.com.

www.ingramcontent.com/pod-product-compliance
Lightning Source LLC
Chambersburg PA
CBHW071447150426
43191CB00008B/1266